T0283918

micrographia micrographia micrographia micrographia micrographia micrographia micrographia micrographia micrographia micrographia micrographia

jennifer bowering delisle

GORDON HILL
PRESS

Edited by Shane Neilson
Cover and book design by Jeremy Luke Hill
Proofread by Carol Dilworth
Set in Linux Libertine
Printed on Mohawk Via Felt
Printed and bound by Arkay Design & Print

LIBRARY AND ARCHIVES CANADA CATALOGUING IN PUBLICATION

Title: Micrographia / Jennifer Bowering Delisle.
Names: Delisle, Jennifer Bowering, 1979- author.
Identifiers: Canadiana (print) 2023044153X | Canadiana (ebook) 20230441548 |
    ISBN 9781774220948 (softcover) | ISBN 9781774220955 (PDF) |
    ISBN 9781774220962 (EPUB)
Subjects: LCGFT: Essays.
Classification: LCC PS8607.E4844 M53 2023 | DDC C814/.6—dc23

Gordon Hill Press gratefully acknowledges the support of the Canada Council for the Arts, the Ontario Arts Council, and the Ontario Book Publishing Tax Credit.

Gordon Hill Press respectfully acknowledges the ancestral homelands of the Attawandaron, Anishinaabe, Haudenosaunee, and Métis Peoples, and recognizes that we are situated on Treaty 3 territory, the traditional territory of Mississaugas of the Credit First Nation.

Gordon Hill Press also recognizes and supports the diverse persons who make up its community, regardless of race, age, culture, ability, ethnicity, nationality, gender identity and expression, sexual orientation, marital status, religious affiliation, and socioeconomic status.

Gordon Hill Press
130 Dublin Street North
Guelph, Ontario, Canada
N1H 4N4
www.gordonhillpress.com

*For the mothers lost and the mothers who have lost,
and for all the women whose dreams of motherhood
have not yet been realized.*

And, as always, for my family.

Contents

Authors's Note

In November of 2016, my mother accessed Canada's new Medical Assistance in Dying (MAiD) program, after several years of pain and progressive deterioration from the degenerative neurological disease multiple system atrophy, or MSA. Some of the essays in this book tell my story as the daughter of a terminally ill patient who accessed MAiD prior to its contentious expansion in 2021.

This work is not intended either to support or condemn the legislation or my mother's choice to access it, but simply an account of my loss and an attempt to honour my mother's memory. I do not speak for my mother, but only for myself.

No one should ever feel like their lives are not valued, or should feel pressured to die because of poverty, isolation, or indignity. I stand with activists fighting for accessibility, equity, improved financial and social support for those with disabilities, and for recognition that disabled lives are lives worth living.

Jennifer Bowering Delisle
Edmonton, 2022

Micrographia

Sometimes what Mom had written was so small she could not even read it herself. She told me this with curiosity, amazement, as if she was describing a museum exhibit or an episode of *The Nature of Things*.

Micrographia: tiny writing, common in certain degenerative neurological disorders. Damage to the basal ganglia, the part of the brain that controls fine motor movement, leads to an inability to scale motion, to regulate the force of muscles. Patients may be unable to keep their words in a straight line. Letters cramp together, their width and height often diminishing over the course of a writing task. This was one of the first symptoms.

*

At a sidewalk stall beneath a blue tarp a woman writes names on rice. First, she presses a grain into a pad of clay to hold it steady. Then she scrapes the surface with a utility knife to remove any ridges. With a fine tipped pen, she makes tiny block letters in black ink. She seals them in vials of coloured oil to both preserve and magnify.

*

Just before I moved back home to Edmonton, Mom told me on the phone that Dad wanted her to see a neurologist. I balked. Dad always imagined the worst case, always made the scene a drama. But when I arrived in her kitchen, I watched her, washing a dish like she was slowly stroking it to sleep.

"Are you okay, Mom?"

"Oh yeah, I'm just tired."

Dad had sat her at the kitchen table and made her touch her nose with the tip of her finger. He observed the tremor in her hands as both partner and physician. He noted the slowness in her movements, like she was underwater. He thought the worst case, and kept it to himself, waiting for her appointment with the specialist.

*

Micrographia is prevalent in Multiple System Atrophy (MSA), once known as Shy-Drager syndrome. MSA is a rare neurological disorder characterized by the degeneration of nerve cells in specific areas of the brain. Involuntary functions such as blood pressure, urine production, and digestion are impaired. Parkinsonism is usually the initial sign, including slowness of movement (bradykinesia), muscle rigidity, poor balance, and tremor—Parkinson's being not just a disease in itself, but an adjective for other ones—*parkinsonian.*

There is no definitive test for MSA. It is distinguished from Parkinson's by autonomic dysfunction and poor response to levodopa. The progression is more rapid, with the patient's ability to walk, talk, eat, and breathe each becoming more impaired. A diagnosis requires waiting, to see if drugs help, to see what falters next.

*

Rice writing began in ancient Anatolia, where rice was a symbol of prosperity. Artisans used a single hair to inscribe verses of the Qur'an.

Ancient micrographia wasn't restricted to rice. One-inch square Assyrian cuneiform tablets date back 4000 years. The phrase "in a nutshell" comes from a copy of *The Iliad* contained within the shell of a walnut, described by Pliny in his 77 C.E. *Naturalis Historia.* Near Jerusalem, scrolls the size of an eye inscribed with Hebrew blessings have been discovered inside amulets dating from the 7th Century B.C.E. Biblical scholars think the tiny words weren't meant to be read. The wearer simply knew they were there, felt the words at their neck when they leaned, heard their messages with the collar bones.

*

When I was growing up, the kitchen table was scattered with notes: phone messages for Dad, reminders to go to the bank or the drycleaner, grocery lists. They were rarely for me, but Mom's writing was evidence of her stabilizing presence in my world. One Christmas, when I was starting to doubt, I remember recognizing her handwriting on the note that Santa left: *Merry Christmas, thanks for the cookies.* She had tried to disguise it, but there was something in her hand that still came through, like a scent on the page.

Even now, I recognize her writing. The same elegant slant that made me ask her, when I was getting married, to address the envelopes for the invitations—her handwriting as precise and pretty as any printer. Though it unwinds a little, I know it, read it with her voice in my head. Her hand, just small, like she is trying to fit a recipe on a single card.

*

In 1665, English physicist Robert Hooke published *Micrographia: Or Some Physiological Descriptions of Minute Bodies Made by Magnifying Glasses.* Using the microscope of his own invention, he made detailed drawings of the louse, the blue fly, the flea—creatures whose anatomy had been hidden by the limitations of human sight. He observed the hair of a deer, the structure of cork. The book originated the word "cell" as a biological unit.

He observed writing under the microscope, too. He found that printed periods were rarely circular, distorted by the grain of the paper whether made by hand or printing press. The inky snarl he illustrated in copperplate is furred, tentacled.

He examined the miniature Bible verses of the day that were printed in the "bredth of a two-pence" for keeping on one's person. Though somewhat illegible to the naked eye, he found that the words were all there, as claimed.

*

MSA can only be definitively identified by autopsy, with microscopes not dissimilar from Hooke's. Scars of alpha synuclein appear like rust spots on the glass. The substantia nigra is pale;

astrocytes increase where neurons have died, like dark spiders, like Hooke's hairy, bestial periods.

*

There is a man in Russia named Andrew Rykovanov who has chiselled a copy of Pushkin's self-portrait along with the text of his poem "Talisman" onto a rice grain.

> Shield thee, love, from evil preying,
> From new heart-wounds—that it can,
> From forgetting, from betraying
> Guards thee this my talisman.

Others inscribe alphabets on chickpeas, nuts, spaghetti.

*

Every Sunday she makes family supper: roast pork or baked salmon, three or four different vegetables, sautéed or steamed, trickled with vinaigrette.

"Mom, you don't need to make so many different dishes."

"Mom, let me bring something."

We begin to buy her tools to make things easier. A light Japanese chef's knife. A garlic crusher that rocks back and forth across the cutting board. But I try not to watch her struggling with the knife, the jars; I try not to take over, the way I try not to pass my infant son the toy he is learning how to reach. She and the baby are on the floor together, both on their hands and knees, and neither of them can crawl. She doesn't want help to stand; she holds her hand out for balance but also to hold us back, her foot slowly twisting beneath her to push against the floor.

*

After the onset of symptoms, almost 80% are disabled within five years. On average, death occurs after 7.9 years. Few live more than a decade.

*

Waseem Rahim, an artist in Karachi, can paint the flags of fifty-five countries on a sewing needle with his naked eye. In Russia, Salavat Fidai carves sculptures of people and mythical creatures into the leads of pencils. Turkish artist Hassan Kale paints scenes of Istanbul on butterfly wings and pepper seeds.

*

When I was little, I could see from my bed the light of her makeshift studio in the guest room, where she painted into the night. Her older brother had always been the artist in the family; painting and drawing were his things. But as a young mother here in Alberta, thousands of miles from her family in Newfoundland, she was now free to explore. She painted her children and scenes from home, experimented with pastel and oil and watercolour, played with colour and composition.

A young art student she found on Kijiji has come to buy her easel. She offers me her old canvases: me and my brother as toddlers in the bath; me reclined with a book, my ponytail hanging over the arm of the sofa. When she painted these, she was younger than I am now. I am late to start my family, after grad school, then years of trying and miscarriages. When she first got sick, all I could think was, I need to have a baby while my mother can still hold one.

*

Willard Wigan of Birmingham carved an image of a motorcycle on a hollowed-out hair stubble using diamond fragments. The sculpture can only be seen with a microscope and is smaller than a human blood cell. Wigan works between the beats of his heart to keep his hands steady for his tiny work.

*

The trainer who used to make her do reps of triceps extensions has her writing on lined looseleaf, tells her to concentrate on touching the top and bottom of each letter to the lines. She shows me the exercises, like I once showed her my homework. The words are big, round and looping.

When I first moved out, she started writing plays. The first were solo spoofs in the Fringe; later she wrote ambitious historical dramas—the shipwreck her grandmother survived, a slant biography of Emily Carr. She had taught me, long before, the foundations of writing. The lines and loops of the alphabet, the rules of grammar, the value of stories—of hearing them, tucked in her arm in my bed. Of telling them, the ones that were made up and the ones that were true.

She has seen two neurologists, and next month she will fly to Toronto to see another. When her tremor is bad, Dad reminds her to take her pill. But there is no cure, no treatment to stop the progression of the disease, only medicine that helps manage the symptoms. A few months after she started Sinemet she tried to stop taking it, convinced that she wasn't sick, that it was the drug itself that was causing her decline. Now she is beginning to accept the truth. Home Care comes to assess the condo and makes recommendations on where to install a grab bar beside the bed. They ask her to show them how she gets in and out of the shower.

The trainer also has her stacking napkin rings on the paper towel holder. Practising swinging her arms again when she walks.

*

As the disease progresses, a patient's systems will break down. Injuries caused by falls are common due to hypotension, loss of balance, and muscle weakness. Patients are eventually unable to leave their beds and may lose their ability to speak. As swallowing becomes more difficult, they may need their food to be pureed, and eventually require a feeding tube. Most will need a tracheostomy to breathe. Pneumonia, choking, and pulmonary embolus are frequent causes of death.

*

In 2003, Pawan Sinha dreamed he inscribed the Baghavad Gita on a single grain of rice while napping at an academic conference. When he awoke, he began making calculations. He worked with his wife and another researcher to eventually print a much longer text, the entire New Testament, on a 5mm square silicone chip, which became the world's smallest book. The words must be enlarged 600 times to be read with the naked eye.

*

One of the worst symptoms so far for my mother is what they call emotional incontinence. The telltale wet spot of tears that she finds incredibly embarrassing. She was always one to cry at commercials, but now the tears flow hot and fast without warning, with even less reason. So stupid, she says, trying to hide her flushed face and the choke in her voice. I don't know why I am crying.

But inside her is all the grief and anger and fear that she holds at bay in order to go on living. She buys a cane with a pretty black and white pattern to best match her wardrobe. She orders a new electric bed. She holds her grandson when she is secure in a chair and reads him a storybook that he tries to shove in his mouth. When he was new, he cried when she held him, as if he felt the unsteadiness in her arms. Now he climbs all over her, grabs for her earrings, unaware that she can't catch him if he lunges for the floor, and this time is short and it is a gift.

*

The woman beneath her tarp does not paint the minarets of Istanbul, but she is as delicate as a surgeon, and quick. The tiny letters appear beneath her pen in sharp slants.

You could do this, Mom. Get a needle, rent a table on the Fringe grounds. Ask the people who stop to spell their names. As you work you will tell them a story about the artisans of ancient Anatolia, about cuneiform letters carved with reeds. The people who gather will see the history in your hands: the wrinkles just beginning to appear, the slender fingers that swaddled and caressed your babies. The scent of garlic and the stains of paint and ink from all the stories you have told. They will see your tremor steady between the beats of your heart.

They will see how much can be said with the smallest of words.

I. Gater

Spectre

That first month, we went to Wreck Beach. Wreck had the best waves, the illusion of open sea, and I was trying to find comfort in the certainty of tides. Everywhere were bodies asking to be looked at. Hipsters with tattoos where pubes were waxed away, old men with bellies brown as nests sheltering bald pink penises. Everywhere bodies who were born. Everywhere the potential to procreate. I was trying to find comfort in the commonplace of life.

I don't know if the fear triggered that first month of trying was because I had expected to be pregnant, or all along expected I might never be. I watched the waves, inched back as the tide came in. Beneath my towel alone a thousand billion grains of sand. My disappointment was unreasonable, my anxiety irrational. We had only just begun. Next month we would try again.

*

Mary Tudor tried to produce an heir. This is what the books say: Mary I, "Bastard Queen," had to pass papist England to a Catholic son, to keep the realm from the hands of heretics. She was expected to do so, and she herself expected to do so. Such royals are not permitted love, or loss.

In September of 1554, both Mary and England thought that she was pregnant. The nursery was readied, she said she felt the baby move. Letters announcing the birth were prewritten with *fil*, which could easily be changed to *fille* if it were a girl. In April, false rumours of a son spread across Europe. But by summer there was no child, her belly receded, and no one in court was allowed to speak of it.

*

As the first year passed, I wondered if my fear had come from a deep knowing, or if it had become a self-fulfilling prophecy. I tried to take control by buying paraphernalia: basal thermometers, ovulation predictor kits, multivitamins, sperm propelling lubricants. They were ways to pass the time. Until, one autumn morning, the awaited surprise—stain of pink on the stick, pink of a pudgy cheek, a tiny mitten, a promise to make me a mother too.

*

Mary was a brutal ruler, burning hundreds of Protestants at the stake. Mary by the Grace of God, Queen of England, Defender of the Faith, Bloody Mary. Call her name three times and she will appear in the mirror, screaming and covered in blood. A game I played with other kids once, twelve and drunk on Pepsi in basement sleeping bags.

Italian psychologist Giovanni Caputo tested the Bloody Mary trick at the University of Urbino. In a room lit by a 25 watt bulb, he placed study participants in front of a mirror, then asked them what they saw after ten minutes of gazing at their own faces. Two thirds saw their reflections deformed. Caputo published his findings in a 2010 paper in the journal *Perception*: "The disappearance or attenuation of face traits," he wrote, "could be linked to the Troxler fading that occurs in the periphery while staring at a central fixation."

*

Before the thing inside becomes a fetus, it is called a fetal pole, just a thickening of cells on the yolk sac's edge. Ours, beneath the technician's searching wand, was too small to measure. Theoretical—fetal pole, north pole. Come back in two weeks, she said, frowning. Wait and see.

*

As we stare at ourselves, Caputo found, distortions in our facial recognition system make us change into something else. A parent's face (18%), an archetypal face (28%), an animal such as a cat, pig, or lion (18%), a monstrous being (48%). But in the mirror

12

we see either what we expect or something terrifying; there can be no in between.

*

My body haemorrhaged after each miscarriage, hurling blood as if enraged. The size of the tissue left behind so small when it was finally extracted that the doctors couldn't believe it could cause this river. Yet the gore was proportionate to my fear. Another year passed; another child passed. Each time what I had thought would be my future seemed more spectral, a monstrous trick of fatigue and shadow.

*

In 1558, Mary again thought that she was pregnant, as a tumour filled her lap. No one believed her, and her husband returned to Spain. There would be no Catholic heir, there would be no child. On her deathbed, blind and feverish, she described to her servants the singing angel children she had seen in her dreams.

Call her name three times and she will appear in the mirror. Say *I stole your baby, Bloody Mary*, and she will reach through the glass.

*

This time, the thickening has become a heart, a head. The picture hangs above my desk: grey face, each vertebra clear, stacked along the bottom of my womb. Still, I am suspicious of my body, the gold flecks of colostrum, the deep purple strokes above my hips. My belly squirms, like a bag of kittens weighed with stones.

"The strange-face illusion may be explained," writes Caputo, "by disruption of the process of binding of traits (eyes, nose, mouth, etc.) into the global Gestalt of face." We see the parts and cannot make a complete picture. In time, when we look, we expect only to see the ghost.

*

But I remember other childish tricks, too. Softer ones, sweeter ones. Wave a pencil fast and loosely in your fingers and it will turn to rubber. When it snows at night, look straight up into the

13

sky; the falling flakes will look like stars rushing past, like you are a rocket, or superman. Hold your arms up.

There is something growing inside me, unnamed limbs distorting my belly. Every day I must choose again, to believe in him.

Someday soon he will appear to me, pig or lion or child. Someday, maybe, I will show him how the berries turn his tongue blue, to spin until he sees the world is moving. How to laugh at these illusions. How, at night, the lights of the ski hills look like satellites, floating miles above the sea.

Premature Burial

Our blue couch cushions are perfect for fort building. The babysitter helps my brother and me construct an epic tunnel that winds around the coffee table, past the chair, across the world. I am first to scramble inside, excited that the living room could become a secret passage or underground lair. Then slowing, hearing myself breathe. The air is hot and smells of old carpet. The heavy cushions, perfectly placed, emit no light. Every sound is muffled. The fabric ceiling gropes at my back, the walls are closing, the foam is a coffin. Can't move, can't breathe—contorted faces of soccer fans mashed against chain link, mashed onto the newspaper's front page. Backseat of the little two-door, people piling in and in—*wait*! I need to get out! Clawing the walls in the pitch-black motel room off a rural highway still dreaming graves and I'm bursting out of the tunnel, cushions flying toward my babysitter, my little brother mad I wrecked it, panting the cool air of the room.

I call it claustrophobia. But it isn't just small spaces, it is anything that might trap me or restrict my movement. When it strikes, rational thought evaporates. There is only panic. Racing heart, shallow breath, my body scrambling, kicking, pushing to get out.

They used to think phobias were caused by a childhood trauma. But most phobic people can't identify a single event as the source of their fear—I remember the fort as the first time, but not the cause. Sometimes phobias are passed down through generations, as children observe the fear in their parents, and adopt it for themselves. There are even theories that chemical changes in the DNA generated by a trauma can cause phobias to be passed down genetically. But the origins are rarely clear.

Growing up, I always knew my mother was claustrophobic. But I can't remember a time when I saw her panic. She was fine in elevators and planes—as I am—we rode many together. Her fear was never an obvious barrier to her everyday functioning. Still, it was there. It may be that our genes carry her grandfather's memory of being buried alive in a collapsed trench in France. It may be that my body took on her anxiety like a gesture, a tilt of the head, a timbre in the voice.

*

I have bought a cognitive behavioural therapy workbook written by two psychologists to help people overcome phobias. The process involves subjecting yourself to the fear stimulus to slowly reduce the fear response. Therapists call this method *exposure*, and the desired outcome *extinction*, meaning the extinction of the fearful association, not of species, not of life. Still, the term is unsettling.

I am to begin simply by imagining the fearful situation and recording my thoughts in that moment. I start googling stories of confinement for inspiration, and soon find myself down a narrow rabbit hole of suitable horrors. Imagine it: in ancient Rome, a vestal virgin who broke her vow of chastity was dressed like a corpse, sent down a ladder into a tiny underground vault with a little food and water, and then the entrance was filled with dirt.

My thoughts... *No escape. No one will hear me.*

Sixteenth-century Germany, children immured in the foundation of castles, so that their innocence would protect its stone. Persia at the beginning of the twentieth century, thieves were walled inside stone pillars, calling for water for days until they died in their desert ovens.

I can't breathe.

The Victorians were obsessed with the nightmare of being buried alive. Cholera sometimes plunged people into comas so resembling death that they did not awaken until the soil hit the top of the coffin. To avoid their nightmare, some wrote in their wills that they should be buried with pistols or poison; others asked for decapitation. The Society for the Prevention of People Being Buried Alive advocated that death be confirmed by waiting for putrefaction. To illustrate the gravity of the problem, doctors William Tebb and Edward Vollum claimed in *Premature Burial and How it May be Prevented* that when cemeteries have been moved, "bodies have been found turned upon their faces, the limbs contorted, with hair dishevelled, the clothing torn, the flesh mutilated, and coffins broken by the inmates in their mad endeavour to escape after returning consciousness, to terminate life only in unspeakable mental and physical agonies."

My thoughts... my thoughts are not in the shape of words. There is only my heart pounding as if it is trying to break free of its cage of ribs.

But these stories are distant, sick fantasies of ancient past. Something closer, then.

After an earthquake in Pakistan in 2005, three boys survived five days buried in the ruins of their school. They lay flat on their backs in the dark with the ceiling touching their noses. In Haiti in 2010, Evans Monsignac was trapped for 27 days in the rubble of a marketplace, and drank sewage to stay alive.

And stayed alive.

My thoughts...

I am terrified of my own fear, that I would not have the strength to survive, the willingness. More terrified that I would survive anyway, that I would have to endure this panic without end.

*

Our fear response is driven by our amygdala, the almond residing in the medial temporal lobe. It receives signals—sounds, smells, touch—and prepares the body to freeze, fight, or flee. Our heart pumps blood to clenching muscles, our lungs take in more air to propel escaping legs.

But the amygdala is not smart, lacking reason and logic. Its memories are that of an animal, the lost foothold on the bank, the predator's paw. It tells our skin to sweat, our pulse to race, and then it receives those signals back again—the skin is sweating, the pulse is racing, so the danger must be real, extreme, now.

Even if specific phobias aren't coded in our DNA, it is likely that genetics predispose people to developing them. In 1971, psychologist Martin Seligman proposed the theory of "preparedness," which posits that evolution has hardwired humans to develop fears of things that once regularly threatened our survival: the dark, where a predator might lurk. The cave that might not have an escape. There is little reason for humans to still fear these things. But for those of us who do, our minds are simple as those that had not yet discovered fire.

*

I decide to see a psychologist who specializes in Cognitive Behavioural Therapy (CBT) for anxiety disorders, including phobias. I meet her in her large downtown office. The room is bright and inviting. The winter sun through the window is as yellow and diffuse as her hair as she shuffles through her paperwork. She scans the anxiety questionnaire I filled out in advance. She asks how the phobia interferes with my everyday life.

"It doesn't too much," I begin. "But once in a while I'm in a situation where it's triggered, and then I completely panic." I am calm, clinical describing this. She writes it all down. Suddenly I feel silly for being here—most of her patients have debilitating anxieties that keep them from working or affect their relationships. I admit that I'm a writer, and I want to write about the process.

"It's good to have a motivation," she says, peering above her reading glasses. "Exposure therapy isn't easy." She asks me whether I agree with certain beliefs. "There isn't enough air in small rooms."

"No."

"I will die."

"Not really."

"I won't be able to cope."

"Yes."

"Oh, you have that belief?" she says, looking up.

Isn't that why I'm here?

She asks me to come back with a list of potential triggers, and the level of fear I estimate they evoke on a scale of 1-100. The enclosed waterslide my son dragged me down—50. The back row of the minivan with the seat folded up—60. I should try to find ones that can actually be duplicated in her office. That evening, my husband is full of ideas. "You would fit inside of my old hockey bag... Or bring a sheet and tell her to roll you up in it; you won't be able to move at all!"

Phobics know that our fear is irrational and excessive, but we tend toward certain cognitive biases. 'Overestimation' means that we predict negative outcomes related to our fear, regardless of their likelihood. We tend to dwell on stories that confirm our predictions, and ignore the statistics that show their improbability. 'Catastrophizing' means we see situations as horrific or unbearable when they are not. We assume that we will not be able to manage them.

The psychologist said that until my next appointment I should keep going with 'imaginal exposures'—imagining a situation to evoke the fear response. So I watch YouTube videos of firefighter trainees, weighed down with heavy coats and oxygen tanks, their goggles blocked out with waxed paper. They must scuttle through a concrete tube the length of a city block. They must navigate a narrow passage webbed with electrical wires, keep going when the ceiling drops on them. Imagine it: the mask on my face, the heavy helmet, the hot Kevlar.

Videos of extreme caving. Spelunkers wriggle through spaces close as t-shirts, deeper into dark tunnels, pushing oxygen tanks ahead of them, contorting around boulders. Lionel's Hole. The Lobster Pot. The Devil's Arse. The Birth Canal. The space is too narrow for the depth of his spine to his breastbone. He wriggles sideways, folding his shoulder in, hugging the rock that impedes his progress.

People do this for *fun*.

But a few minutes into the video, my pulse normalizes, my breath deepens, and I am free to watch with fascination rather than terror. He slides on his back, lying in a few inches of silty water, the rock face threatening his chin. And then he is out, donning again the helmet that he'd removed to fit his head through the narrowest spots. There is no cathedral adorned with stalactites and crystals, just a space big enough to turn around, and go back again. The payoff is just in squeezing through.

"Even after the phobia has gone away, you're never really cured," the psychologist says matter-of-factly. "If I helped you overcome a fear of flying, and then you didn't get on another plane for a year, the phobia would return." She draws a little diagram on the whiteboard behind her. "We can teach you to find a new pathway between the stimulus and the brain. But that fear pathway will always still exist."

Back to YouTube. News stories of drivers trapped in vehicles, interred in distorted steel, whose rescuers had to use the Jaws of Life. I don't care about the "of life" part—it is the terror inscribed in "jaws," in the necessity of their existence. The in-between, the critical limbo, smell of blood and gasoline, airbag caul, waiting for a firefighter to pry apart the tomb.

I find a video demonstration—crushed metal spread on an enormous blue tarp on a sunny summer day. The Jaws of Life use hydraulics to pop door panels, peel back the steel like a banana, lift dashboards. I watch them shear off a roof in two minutes. Totalled cars bloom beneath the machines. Could I wait that long? Ten minutes to arrive, two to get me out. Would the panic do what the crash had not? Or could I have the capacity to wait, to choose to survive?

If you are confident that you can handle the exposure, it won't be effective. You have to be unsure. The key to exposure is embracing the fear.

The psychologist zips me into my down winter coat with my arms tight to my body instead of through the sleeves. It's hot. I can't move. It's just a coat, and I feel silly standing there. But I *really really* want to get out.

"What's your number?"

"40."

"That's a good place to start. What would make the number higher?"

You can't talk yourself down because you're already aware that it's irrational. Instead, you have to train your amygdala to respond to the stimulus differently. You have to invite the fear in, feel it until it passes, until your whole brain knows there is no danger. You have to do it again and again.

*

I am in the waiting room in a hospital, my mother is beside me. She pulls a snack for us to share out of her purse. Then I realize that I am waiting to have an MRI. I am already lying on the table, sliding into the tunnel. Just as the machine begins to swallow me, I wake up, sweaty and gasping.

I don't need an MRI.

My mother would never have had a can of cocktail wieners in her purse.

And she has been dead for two years.

This was a dream. But it takes an hour for my panic to ease enough that I can go back to sleep.

In the last year of her life, my mother would often wake in the night locked in her body. She couldn't roll, or turn her head, couldn't press the call button in her hand, couldn't call out. The nurses began to wake her up in the night for an extra dose of Sinemet to try to stop what is known as 'locking in.' But the irrational phobia that my mother once suffered had become a legitimate fear. She was exposed to her fear again and again, and the danger was real.

I tell the therapist about my dream. "An MRI is a pretty common diagnostic test," I say. "I could be hit by a car and need one tomorrow." I haven't told her about my mother's illness and death, I realize. It hadn't seemed relevant—I was always claustrophobic, long before my mother got ill, since I was a child.

She looks at me skeptically. "The fear of something that *could* happen is enough to make you seek treatment? You'll probably go your whole life and never need an MRI."

I don't know what to say to this. I am at once indignant at her dismissal and embarrassed at what must seem like my trivial complaint. How to explain, the fear of it is enough, the fear itself is overwhelming. How to explain this if she, of all people, doesn't understand it already?

In my dream, my mother could move, she wasn't sick at all.

    *

A year or two into her illness, new research suggested that MSA is caused by a newly discovered prion, not a trip-switch inherited in the genes. We discussed it around the dinner table one Sunday, academically, matter-of-factly, knowing that the discovery didn't explain why she had it, that it would mean nothing for her treatment or the progression of the disease that had her sitting with her mouth open, waiting for my dad to put the fork in. Prions are infectious proteins that cause the abnormal folding of similar proteins, causing lesions in the brain. Like Mad Cow Disease. The dark joke that made her laugh: we can only get MSA from Mom if we eat her.

Darker still was my secret relief. Maybe there was not a death sentence written in my DNA. Maybe I would be saved from not only the physical pain, the early death, but from being entombed in my own body. From awakening in the dark of my own mind.

*

My mother stretched the limits of what she could bear, to see her grandchildren grow for another month, to be pushed in her wheelchair to a café one more Saturday afternoon, and watch people walk by. She was not the romantic stoic whose story is told for someone else's inspiration. She was angry. She was terrified. And she knew that her symptoms would worsen until her death.

In the last months of her life, I was witness to much of her suffering. It was not that she couldn't feel her body—she felt it more acutely. Every muscle in her neck, every joint in her limbs, screamed in pain. But when she was locked in, she was alone.

Imagine it. The room is dark. The call button is in her hand but she can't press it—her thumb doesn't receive her brain's garbled signal. In the distance, she can hear a nurse's footfall, another resident whimper. But they are as far from her as the moon. Her voice is as muffled as if she were immured in stone. She lies there in the dark, and when it is over, she is still alive.

Isn't that, then, why I am here? Zipped up in my winter coat?

My thoughts: there is no reason to think that the same thing will happen to me. And yet, there is every reason to be afraid.

Gator

There are alligators in Disney World. Not the kind that eat alarm clocks and pirate hands, not pickpocket euphemisms. The kind that will drag a two-year-old wading on the beach into the lagoon and hold him under water until he drowns.

*

My two-year-old has books with alligators. Gators that make soup and pie, that drive cars. In his books they are friends with bears, they wear pants and paint pictures. This is what the letter A is for.

*

The story dominates the news. The alligator may have mistaken the toddler for an armadillo, its normal prey. Sightings had been reported, insufficient signage. The resort knew. Eighteen-hour search, body intact. Five alligators removed from the property, two over six feet long.

*

There is a game we play in my son's Music and Motion class. The children hold the edge of a parachute and stick their feet underneath. We sing a song, naming their body parts as we pull the parachute up, over their knees, over their bellies. We sing that we're being swallowed by a wolf. Over their shoulders, over their heads. They scream with glee.

The parents hold the parachute up, waving triangles of red, blue and yellow light. Dead is under the ground, rabbit in a burrow. The bellies of animals are bright red rooms.

*

The boy had been building a sand castle. He must have had a bucket and shovel, soapy smell of SPF60. The father who jumped in the water and tried to pry open the jaws had been in the sand beside him moments before. Maybe he taught the boy the word 'turret.' Maybe he sat on his sandals, said, "Don't put sand in your hair." In the photo on the news the child wears a sweater, so he is in a sweater on the beach in my mind, getting sand stuck in the wool, wet cuffs.

*

Does my son notice my goosebumps? Can he smell my fear, the primal, pheromone stink of it? Could he hear it in my voice, calling his name in the store while he hid in the small dusty corner where the shelves didn't quite meet? Testing it, like a hot pan with his fingertip, learning the relationship between action and reaction, learning his power and my powerlessness. Laughing.

We don't need goosebumps to make our hair stand up, to make our bodies seem bigger to the scary movie, the news story. Yet there are thousands of years of evolution in this, our skin's small reminder that we were once meat. What a small adaptation, even when we had a coat of hair. How weak that seems in the face of jaws and scales.

*

An American mother known as SM does not experience fear because of damage to her amygdala. Psychologists have been studying her for twenty years. Because she does not avoid dangerous situations, she has been held at knife and gunpoint more than once, repeatedly physically assaulted and threatened with death. To test if she really lacks fear, the researchers take her to an exotic pet store, where she must be stopped from poking the deadly reptiles. I don't know why they don't try telling her that her children are in danger.

*

There are other stories that you hear, on the radio, around the office. The toddler who wandered out in the snow. The car crash. The babysitter who left the children and went shopping.

The woman who forgot her grandson in the car one summer afternoon. My husband starts the story, as if to release it from his mind, then stops. "You don't want to know." But then, I must know, must hear the end. The more common dangers, the closer losses. I have to hear them before I can lock them away in the darkest corners of my imagination.

*

The average alligator is thirteen feet long. They have been known to balance on hind legs to lunge. Their mouths hold eighty teeth.

*

An alligator pull-toy with wheels. A stuffed gator playing the banjo. A sprinkler gator that sits in the grass. We give children these toys to intertwine the dread encoded in our genes with soft things, silly things, games. Because we still fear the animals. Because we know it's not the animals we really need to fear.

*

I chase my son's small pink body down the hall, flesh shiny from the bath, with his pyjamas in my hand. Gator on the shirt, and green bottoms that say, "No Swimming."

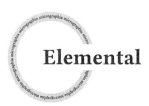

Elemental

The smell of raw beef—your head beneath my chin. You have stopped crying now, but my body still reverberates. Your wails (crying is good), and before that, your father's desperate NO! NO! NO! between the thuds of head on stair treads, as if he could command gravity, stop your body midair. The sound of my husband watching our child—

But you didn't. You cried, at the bottom.

You hold a little blue car in your hand. When we first sat down in the waiting room a man offered it to you from the pocket of his jean jacket. He didn't speak, seemed unable to. He seemed lost, mute and childless in the ER of the children's hospital. Odd, but not threatening. The car smelled strongly of cigarettes, as though it had been in his pocket a long time. Through your cries I said thank you, a question in my voice, but he walked away, left the building through the sliding glass doors.

We chat with other parents, in calm tones, as in an elevator or the park. A mosquito allergy has swollen a tween girl's eye closed. A toddler has an abscess in his mouth. While the metal smell in my nose explains, iron, oxygen—the elements that let you live heralding themselves, soaking through the stack of napkins grabbed off the counter, dripping down on the new shirt that you love with the polar bear playing hockey. While I see what I did not see, your body looping in space, a molecule suspended in a textbook diagram.

When you shift to your father's lap I take the car to the bathroom and wash it in the sink, but the cigarette smell stays, locked in the metal. A toy that reeks like grown-up places and grown-up poisons. A toy without a child.

You want to see the fish in the aquarium. We watch the little clowns wander through coral, watch a snail streak up the glass. By the time we see the doctor, the blood in your hair and on my shoulder is long dry. It is 1 a.m., but you are bright, answering her questions. You did not lose consciousness, you did not vomit. You know your name, and something of what happened. The split along your scalp is straight and holding closed—no need even for stitches, though you will always have a thin white scar where your hair does not grow, a reminder I will see, months from now, when you are sitting down at the table, or playing on the floor, when the smell of raw meat is the hamburger in the bowl and I am impatient with you to wash your hands.

*

At home, we gently wash the blood from your hair with a cloth, ease you into your pyjamas. Tonight, your father will sleep beside you in your narrow bed, for his own comfort more than yours. Tonight, we will allow ourselves to acknowledge the thought that pumps unseen, right beneath the skin, elemental as the heme nestled in its coils.

I find the little car in the pocket of my sweater, and throw it in the garbage. I can't clean the odour off this strange man's kindness. It is too small, too blue, too like the others in the toy box, and I can't imagine it there. Can't imagine it on the race track rug, where you command your own gravity, piloting cars into the sky.

Okay

When my son was barely old enough to speak, he came down with a stomach virus. All night he vomited, wailing "I'm okay" between heaves. "I'm okay!" It was not a reassurance; it was a plea.

I had given him these words. Every time he fell, I comforted him, in a singsong voice: *it's okay, you're okay.* I knew, in my grown-up brain, that the cut would close, that the goose egg would recede, that he was, in fact, okay. I meant to comfort him, and myself. But it was a kind of plea then, too. What I knew in my brain I didn't always know in my pounding heart.

A little older, now, and he knows the names for most of his feelings. And he is learning how to read them—learning that each letter on the page is a sound, that together the sounds make the words. But he has read the books before, completes the sentences with what he thinks is there.

"Sharks have lots of—"

"Teeth!"

"V—v—v—*very*...sh—sharp..."

"Teeth!"

I show him the world the way I show him pictures on my phone, snapshots we can scroll through. A shot of beauty, a shot of silliness, a blurry glimpse of filtered pain.

"If someone tried to hurt me, I would just hit them."

"But that wouldn't solve it, you have to use your words. Sometimes bullies are really just lonely. Maybe you could try to be his friend."

Is this really what I want to teach him? When my child has a nightmare, do I tell him, it was only a dream? Or do I tell him, I understand, you are afraid. I am afraid.

He is listening to the radio, learning the language of the world between the music. He absorbs *justice*. He absorbs *supreme court*. He knows the word *hearing*, it is what his ears do. Like listening, only listening is a word we use when we really mean being bad: *you're not listening.*

What does it mean, then, to be bad? We tell him, you're not bad, you sometimes do bad things. But he sees the world in terms of good guys and bad guys—those with capes and those with sneers. Both have weapons, both have power. "Now *you're* the good guy," he says when we wrestle, yet the game does not change.

It is bad to colour on your face with a marker. It is bad to throw toys, except for balls. It is bad to scream, unless you are hurt or really in danger. It is good to hug when you are sorry— but not always. *Ask your friend first, if it's alright to hug him. When someone says stop, you stop. Your sister doesn't like that— look at her face.*

"Don't worry," he says, "I'm a good shark."

He knows there is no such thing as monsters, as vampires, with coffin beds and hidden fangs, things that could bite our necks, remake us in their image. Things that could challenge the boundaries of being human, make us live forever, make us fly. No, monsters are not real, we have told him so. "Have I ever eaten blood?" he asks one November morning in the car, with the iron taste of winter on his tongue.

We are listening to the radio. I absorb *ruling*, like rules, only there are none. Only rulers. What does it mean to be good? You are good if they believe you are good, if they believe you are good enough, if they believe you over her. You are good if you are a good director, if you are a good novelist. That sitter told him he was a good boy if he didn't cry when his mama left.

He stomps on my foot by accident: "but it's okay," he assures me. He takes his sister's toy, hears her cry. "But it's okay," he sings. "*Iiiiit's* okay." And I am realizing my mistake. I have tried to get him to think about how the other person feels when he does not share, when he hits. But I have neglected to teach him that sometimes you can't know what someone else feels. That sometimes people are not okay; that telling them they are doesn't make it so.

"Why is it so dark?" he asks one November morning. Because, in winter—

In winter, the earth tilts away from the sun, towards the blackness of the universe. We have travelled 470 million kilometres in space since the summer began.

Is this what I need to teach him? "Turn on the lights," my daughter whimpers from her carseat.

Yes, there are bad guys, and good guys. But there are also those who think they're good, who think that everything belongs to them, like children do. Those who tell us it's okay and almost believe it. Those who tell each other it's okay, and do believe it.

It's okay is a warning. It's okay is a gag. It's okay is a callused hand, stroking reassurance across bared skin.

We are listening to the radio. He is listening.

"Do you know that letter? N, what sound does that make? Ne—ne—"

What do I want to teach him?

We don't colour in books, on walls, on our skin. Yet bodies are pages to be read; when you look at them, see that they are already covered in words.

We don't hit or scream unless we are really in danger.

The Dance

When I was very young, I told my mother I wanted to be the next Shakespeare. I don't think I knew that he was a poet. I don't think I even knew his stories were plays. But I loved when she read to me at bedtime from Charles and Mary Lamb's *Tales from Shakespeare*. I had heard phrases like "the greatest writer to have ever lived" and it seemed a worthwhile ambition.

I don't recall the feeling now, only the conversation. Did I want fame? I don't think so. I wanted to make art as compelling as those stories of murderous kings and doomed lovers. I think I wanted greatness, but a greatness formed out of beauty and connection. A love for my words big enough to endure 400 years.

"Well, maybe not *Shakespeare*..." she said.

I didn't understand yet anything of historical context, let alone of the man or the work itself. I didn't know my goal was ludicrous, even obnoxious. What I heard, in her response, was my limitations. It was the beginning of the rite of passage from a child's arrogance to an artist's self-doubt.

*

Mom has decided to remount a play she wrote for the Fringe a few years ago, as a fundraiser for MSA. She busies herself finding a director and a venue and overseeing the casting. It is something to occupy her time and her mind, but it is also a final project, a kind of opus.

The play, *Wind in Her Sails*, tells the story of Mom's grandmother, Jean, who at the age of 16 saved the lives of those onboard a ship that wrecked in a storm off the coast of Newfoundland. I told the same story in my own first book, a family memoir about to be published.

Mom and I portray the event in different ways. In her play, Jean takes the wheel when the captain is knocked out, steering the ship to safety, heedless of the warning that "the wheel be a challenge even fer a strong man, miss." Her play is about the strength—both physical and mental—of young outport women, despite the misogyny of their time. It is a drama in every sense of the word, full of peril and inspiration.

In my non-fiction version, I gather the fragments that live in old newspapers and oral histories, including Jean's own poem about the experience. The stories don't add up. The one from an archive that claims Jean took the wheel, the most exciting and dramatic version of the tale, can't be true. Jean's own poem says the wheel was smashed when the mast fell. My book is about the errors in the record, how we can't ever know the real story.

My mother's is a story about triumph, while mine is a story about inadequacy.

*

In grade four, my teacher invited a few of us in my class to write books to be included in the school library. I had already been writing stories and poems on my own, but this—this would get a laminated cover and pocket for a real borrowing card. It would be read by someone besides my teacher or my mom. I could see it all before me—book deals, bestseller lists, film adaptations. My career as a writer had finally begun.

I began the project with vigour and earnest. I wanted my story to be serious and important, to both move and inspire. I invented a girl, Danielle, the same age as me, whose mother had died and whose father was an alcoholic. Danielle was an earnest, capable girl, trying to take care of her family, like the girls in the books I read. She cooked, she cleaned. She made her father a birthday cake, and knowing vaguely that sometimes cakes were made with rum, I had him raging when he learned his daughter's cake did not contain any booze.

My mother found my half-finished manuscript. After school she sat me down for a talk.

"There's an expression," she said gently. "Write what you know."

My face burned. There was something in this conversation that evoked shame, but I didn't fully understand why.

At first, I thought she was worried that people reading it would think it was a cry for help—that my own father was the abusive alcoholic on the page. I know now there was no danger of that. It could have been a much-needed lesson on my own privilege, appropriation of voice, and staying in my lane. But my mother meant it as a lesson on craft. Emotion is not inherent in plot—it has to come from a deeper place.

I ended up writing something about ghosts.

But I drew from my own life, creating grandparent characters very similar to my own, a detail about a little brother getting stuck in his own shirt, which had happened to mine the week before. I didn't learn the lesson quite right—or maybe I learned it too well—starting to blur the lines between life and writing in a way that would sometimes paralyze me. Did I know this story enough? Who was I to tell it? And if I did feel the emotion deeply enough, could I still write it?

*

I first came to Jean's story because she was a poet. I saw in her ballad's existence a kind of writerly lineage. "It's in the blood," people say when a child exhibits a proclivity for the art or science of their parent. As if that means they have come by their talent more authentically, as if that means their work has more legitimacy.

Yet I know of no other poems or stories, and she never shared the ballad she wrote about the shipwreck, keeping it hidden until her death.

*

Mom sends me a new monologue she has written; she's thinking of having an actor perform it before the play. "When you have time" is the email subject line. It's called "The Dance."

My husband and I love to dance, she writes. *Of course, we don't know what we're doing. I didn't say we dance well...just that we love to dance.*

She writes about abandoning the ballroom classes for their own version of the steps. She writes about her own parents celebrating their 60th anniversary, the night before my wedding—

how they danced in her kitchen, how in the middle of the night her mother, in the fog of Alzheimer's, tried to walk out the front door. And she writes about her MSA.

On a recent cruise, I told my husband that I would love to give dancing a go again.

"I would never do anything that would make us look foolish," *he said.*

So we practised a bit in our state room, because now I use a walker...There we were...Me holding on for dear life to the man I married while he maneuvered me around, until I got dizzy and collapsed on the bed. We never made it onto the dance floor, that night or any other night.

"Is the monologue good enough?" she asks. "To be mounted with *Wind in Her Sails?*"

I understand her question. It's the same one that I would ask. But it's the wrong question, too.

In these last months of your life, Mom, what else do you need to say?

No, forget the timeline, it's irrelevant.

In this one life, what stories do you need heard? What do you want to make?

*

Jean wrote her poem about a single public event. But as I wrote about her, I became less interested in her heroism, real or imagined, and more interested in her life. How she worked, how she loved. Farmed, hooked mats, cooked fish. Lost infants to disease, lost a son in war, lost her mind in age. Kept secrets. Died. What was "in the blood" were her stories; it felt like they were also my stories. I wanted to map her life like a genome. Maybe "write what you know" should be "write what you want to know."

The story I want to tell now is not romanticized by corset or sail, by historical and geographical distance. It is a story that is still unfolding.

I send Mom an essay I have written about her illness, called "Micrographia." I am proud of the craft of it, relieved by the work of it. But is it good enough—to honour what she is going through, to remember? What words could ever be adequate?

*

A boy in my class took my ghost story out of the library.

"It was good," he said. "I liked the part where the kid gets stuck in his shirt. That was funny."

It was good.

*

The same evening Mom emails back. Her email is short but brimming with positive adjectives. "Deep respect and sincere pride in you," she writes. And with that she seems to be gifting me—not the story, which is her life—but this tiny piece of it. She likes it. And maybe this is good enough.

*

"The Dance" ends with my mother dancing with my son.

He pushes my walker...trying to drive it. Sometimes I get behind the wheel and he chases me around the kitchen island.

What dance moves can we do together from my wheelchair?

He doesn't care or even know if he is being judged.

Whirling past like a hurricane. Always smiling.

I can never fully know what my mother is going through. But our stories dance with each other, close, twirling, stepping on the other's toes.

We make art imperfectly, incompletely, as a way of being in the world, hoping that it will be good enough to outlive us. Hoping that it will be good enough to help us share our truth with those who come after us.

Maybe the doubt is what keeps that truth close.

Maybe "write what you know" should be "write what you want to keep."

II. Knowing Another

micrographia micrographia micrographia micrographia micrographia micrographia micrographia micrographia micrographia micrographia micrographia micrographia micrographia micrographia jennifer bowering delisle

Screen Time

My children are watching *PAW Patrol* so I can read Sharon Olds. Curve of simile, more bare than skin, freed verse slipping in and the pups must catch the runaway elephant. Neuroscientists call screens "electronic cocaine" and "digital heroin." And there are dishes in the sink, banana glue beneath the table. Dust bunnies so big my kid could push them in her little stroller. But there is poetry, slow lick of lyric, sibilant, aspirate, the line, the rhythm, spondee, trochee, urging to be heard. The knowing of another, the being known. Research shows screen time raises dopamine to the level of sex, to addiction. That it interferes with the development of the frontal lobe, where we reason, where we control our drives. I am standing with my book in my hand, standing above the breakfast crumbs and little plastic school bus, the pups are luring the elephant with peanuts, and Olds is watching her own children sleep now. Her room is quiet. Her daughter's pouting mouth, her son's bent leg. And her knowing is love and her love is a world, and I know this love, too, its unique friction, its terror, how having everything can feel like asking, always asking. How having everything demands the words, to be written, to be heard.

Abracadabra

It was once a word with power, before hokey top hats and scarves stuffed up sleeves: write it on papyrus eleven times, dropping the final letter on each line. Whatever evil has befallen you will diminish with the word.

*

Abracadabr

On screen our names are not our own: Wannabemama, Hope82. Yet these handles grasp our true selves, as our longing has become our identities. We are anonymous but naked as the animals we are, driven by our most primitive instincts.

We are TTC: trying to conceive. I log in when I should be working, to share with strangers how badly I want a child. And to read how badly they do, too. To read that they are also infected by that single force, which supplants work, relationships, the dinner plate, the steering wheel.

We share the minute details of our efforts, cycle days and basal body temperatures, everything written in a kind of shorthand, as if we have something else to do besides wait, and wait. BFN for "big fat negative" on a home pregnancy test; "DH" for "dear husband;" 2WW for "two week wait," that agonizing time between ovulation and finding out if you are, finally, pregnant. Together these abbreviations become a dialect of their own. A kind of spell. To take the comfort here I have to learn the tongue, to be one of them I have to use it.

*

Abracadab

The source of power is not in the meaning of the words but in their utterance. In antiquity, vowels representing planets and consonants representing elements were combined to make *voces magicae*, nonsense syllables rhymed and metred, sometimes mixed with real words.

The earliest reference to "abracadabra" appears in a text by Serenus Sammonicus, physician to the Roman emperor Caracalla. To treat colds and fevers, Sammonicus prescribed wearing an amulet bearing abracadabra in its diminishing form for ten days. On the morning of the eleventh day, the patient was to rise before dawn and throw the amulet in a river.

*

Abracada

I came to the site looking for a community of women, and reassurance that I am not alone. Nobody else can understand that you can grieve for something you never had. Nobody else knows that a Nerf dart can pierce the skin, the fear of running boots with flashing lights, the assault of onesies on a rack paired with little hats. That a child, small as a loaf of bread, could deliver blows while sleeping in her stroller.

I had always known I wanted to be a mother. But I'm a feminist; I don't believe that women are defined by motherhood, that we need to reproduce to be fulfilled, to be complete. So I was not prepared for the click of my biology, for my want to become need, as physical as thirst. My body has betrayed me twice: by not performing this basic function, and by registering this failure not in my intelligent mind, but in my throat, my gut, my tissues.

*

Abracad

In the thread for women over thirty who have been trying longterm, Sunshine has been here the longest. She's had a miscarriage already. I like her handle—its quiet hopefulness in the midst of all the loss and uncertainty. So I am happy for her when she comes on to share that she has finally conceived again. This is what I need, the happy-ending story of someone like me. She has just taken a little longer; maybe I am just taking a little longer.

It's nice to be happy for Sunshine. I avoid the real women I know who are pregnant. Six of them, right now. Before I was "trying" I had heard of this, how infertile women could be consumed by envy—sneering at strangers, turning on their loved ones—and with my rational, stable mind I had judged them. Now I am one of them. When I see pregnant women, I am curt, quietly excusing myself to go to a bathroom I don't need, unable to summon a smile or friendly chitchat. It isn't really envy. Their joy is a kind of violence.

I want them to be insensitive to me, cruel, even, so that I will have an excuse for the anger I feel.

I want these mothers to know my pain.

It's nice to be happy for Sunshine.

I congratulate Sunshine with as much sincerity as I could have for a stranger. Another woman shares a little emoji with a broom and pointy hat: she is not pregnant this month, her "witch" has come.

*

Abraca

Alfalfa, nettle leaf. Vitamin B6. Green tea and pineapple core. Bhramari breath, feet up the wall, maca root and pomegranates. Drink water lukewarm, menstrual cups to hold the sperm in. Visualize the seed, the egg, see your baby. Have you tried? Worked for me. Made the difference. Couldn't hurt.

*

Abrac

Charms often used homeopathic compounds—invented words that contained the name of the disease the spell sought to cure. Their elusive meanings were proof of their power, the supremacy of the one who wielded them.

Hocus Pocus is said to have started as a corruption of the Latin sacramental phrase, *Hoc est enim corpus meum*, "this is my body," used by jugglers to add gravitas to their illusions.

Abracadabra may derive from Hebrew, *evra k'divra*—I create as I speak. It may be biblical Aramaic, *avra gavra*—I will create man.

*

Abra

I want understanding, commiseration. Wannabemama says my luteal phase, the time between ovulation and the start of menstruation, is too short. And maybe I want that too—maybe on some level I believe that these faceless avatars might give me the answers I haven't found in my doctor's office, that this community of women could share a collective wisdom and find the secret potion.

Any given month, a woman who ovulates normally is fertile for less than 24 hours. In that short window one mobile sperm must survive the acid of the vagina, grope towards the egg and burrow in. One hundred million sperm start that journey, and only about a hundred make it even close to the egg. That's if the man's sperm is healthy. If the egg is fertilized, it must find a spot in the uterus's lining to implant, free of cysts or scars, while hormones prompt the lining to grow thick for the zygote to nestle in. Conception seems like a kind of magic, an unlikely, hopeful wish.

Up to 16% of heterosexual couples experience infertility, depending on how the term is defined. Research suggests that these rates are increasing, possibly due to women delaying childbearing for higher education or to establish a career. As I have done.

*

Abr

Hope82 might be ovulating, and goes into graphic detail about the consistency of her cervical mucous (CM). Though she offers the warning, it is not too much information (TMI). This is the substance we are all obsessed with, another gauge for when we are most fertile. Stretchy and clear like egg whites, we pull it, analyze it, judge it.

Yet in the next sentence she calls her period "AF" for "Aunt Flo," and sex "BD" for "bed dancing." I don't want euphemisms. I don't want to dress my excretions in little bows, giggle at my sex, put sparkles on my pain. I can't offer someone "baby dust," the fairy emoji. I don't want to be made into the child I am missing.

Yet I keep coming back to the site, with its rocking bed emojis and the women whose pets are "fur babies." It's a way of taking my infertility out of my self, making it a thing to read and say and do, instead of a state of being.

The sidebars rotate ads for books and teas, acupuncture to rid yourself of toxins, hypnosis programs to remove your deep psychological barriers. I am tempted to click even through my scepticism, my offence. Could it be that my body is toxic, that I need to just "take charge" of my fertility, that my sympathetic and parasympathetic nervous systems are misaligned, that I have a mental clog, that I really don't want it enough?

*

Ab

Sunshine lost the pregnancy. She just posted—she had been spotting, her doctor has now confirmed it. She reached out to us across cyberspace, grieving—not just the loss of this child but what seems like the loss of her motherhood. I am heartbroken for her. And I am terrified; as I could see in her my own future good fortune, I can see in her my own future losses. I muddle together a response, something awkward and inadequate, but sincere. We are strangers, but I'm here.

A few hours later I am back, scrolling quickly through the posts, looking for the comfort of a shared grief. The other women have offered her emoji hugs, little hearts and perfect blue teardrops. They've said oh no, they've said I'm sorry. And on the same line they've said that they are on day 3 of their 2WW, and felt a little twinge; they've posted pictures of their temperature charts, they've said that they are ovulating so tonight's the night for some BD.

I log off, I close my computer. This is not a place for comfort. This is narcissism dressed up like a community. In our quest to become mothers we have lost ourselves as caregivers. In our focus on our biology we have forgotten our humanity.

Maybe I was naïve to think we could find care on a computer. This is how the site is built, with clickbait and cartoon avatars, dancing storks and flashing hearts, shaping how we write, and connect. Everything telling us that women lack the maturity and intelligence to discuss our own reproduction and infertility frankly, critically. Everything telling us that we are to blame, but the fixes are quick, and for sale. This is sleight of hand, flashes of silk to make us lose sight of what's real.

*

A

I open my computer again, this time to a blank document, and I begin to write. The words I am creating are not a child, they do not satisfy my longing, or even bring me back to the world. But they are beginning to ease the grip of pseudoscience and superstition, that constant worry and hope that my infertility is in my power to change. They are the words I have been yearning to read, the long ones, the phrases, the ones that fill my mouth with flavours sharp and familiar. The ones I know to be true. A new incantation: this is beyond our control. I'm here, I hear you. I know you.

The origin of the word "spell," in both senses, is Germanic—a tale, a story, a history. Here is my tale, that its power over me may diminish with each letter. Here is my story, that it may be read, and recognized. Here is my history, that it may heal.

A Routine Test

Radiology is at the end of the hall, guarded by a receptionist encased in glass and a red machine dispensing numbers. I take one and find a seat in the corner, beside a stand of pamphlets in different languages. I guess at the alphabets. Vietnamese. Korean. *Information for Patients Having an Ultrasound. Information for Patients Having an X-Ray. Information for Patients Having a Hysterosalpingogram.*

The specialist had explained the procedure, but I already knew about it from reading too much on the internet, late night googling of infertility when once again the test came up blank. Month seven, month ten, month twelve. Hysterosalpingogram, or HSG. The radiologist injects a high contrast dye through the cervix, which will show if there are any blockages in the fallopian tubes, any fibroids or polyps, anything that might be preventing me from getting pregnant. The reason why my body has failed this most primordial function. There will be some cramping, the doctor said.

"Number eighteen?"

"I have a 3:00 appointment," I say through the window.

"Do you have your Care Card and picture ID?"

I pass the receptionist the cards, and she types a few things into her computer. Then she passes me a gown and robe.

"There are change rooms behind you. Remove your shirt, the gown opens in the back. If your bra has any metal, it's best to take that off too. You can leave your underwear on for now. Here's a robe to cover yourself. You can have a seat until they call you. But they're running a bit behind today."

The change room looks like a change room at a swimming pool—orange partitions, wooden benches, tile floor. Did she say bra on or off? Should I go back out and ask? They are looking at my uterus, why do I need to take my bra off? I decide to remove it. It will be easier to take it off now than later, I think. I wrap the robe around me and stuff my clothes into my purse.

In the waiting room an elderly gentleman sits stiffly, trying to maintain a distinguished air in his hospital robe. I am wearing more clothing now than when I came in in my t-shirt and shorts, yet I feel more exposed, like that dream that I've worn my pajamas to work. The soft flannel feels wrong against the vinyl of the waiting chairs. Behind the man a sign on the wall reads, *If You are Pregnant Please Inform Us so Precautions Can be Taken.*

Infertility is easy to diagnose. If you don't conceive after a year, you are "infertile." I diagnosed myself. Finding the reason beneath is the hard part. Endometriosis. Polycystic Ovarian Syndrome. Septate Uterus. Premature Ovarian Failure.

I pick up a magazine, flip the pages without reading, letting my eyes slide across the pictures. I thumb my way through once, then back the other direction. I want to check my messages, but stop when I see the large picture of a phone with a big red X through it on the wall.

I watch others come and go, the routine at the window, the pile of clothes. A thirty-something woman with her husband. An old woman with a walker, guided by her middle-aged daughter. I can hear the daughter helping her in the change room behind me. "Here Mum, let me help you take your bra off." I try to distract myself by guessing what they are all here for. An ultrasound, to look at the kidneys. An MRI, to look for tumours. Peeling back the skin and flesh to see what's beneath. They are not here to be fixed, not yet. They are here simply to look, to see what is inside. What is broken, what is blocked, what is causing that pain. Diseases, malformations, degenerations, the secrets our bodies hold even from ourselves. Soon, I will know too.

After half an hour a man comes out of one of the doors and calls a name. The old lady and her daughter stand slowly, then disappear behind a door. I pick up their magazine. *The Two Top Summer Trends: PRINTS and NEUTRALS.* Can these be trends, if together they encompass almost everything? I thumb through it without reading, let it fall closed again on the pale print of my lap. A tiny brown stain interrupts my robe's pattern. Blood? I wonder. Shit?

A pregnant woman comes in and takes a seat. I watch her as she texts someone beneath the no cell phones sign. She is one of those who gets pregnant first try, or by accident. Who posts pictures of her belly on Facebook, along with status updates complaining about her swollen feet. She is my relative, she is my coworker. She is the picture of maternity, with her giant fecund belly, the imprint of her navel just visible under the fabric of her dress, her round breasts about to burst with milk. But she does not know this deep maternal grief, a grief that comes from the most primal inner place I never knew was there.

An hour later the lady in scrubs emerges from the corridor, clipboard in hand, and calls my name. "I'm Marjorie," she says, smiling warmly. "Sorry about the wait."

"No problem," I lie.

I follow her down the hallway, left, then left again. "We're not quite ready for you yet, but I thought I would at least take you down and get you to fill out the form. It's been one of those days!"

Marjorie leads me to a chair in a quiet hallway, outside the HSG room. She hands me her clipboard. "I just took another woman in, and she'll be about fifteen minutes, then it'll take me about five minutes to change over the room. Okay?"

She goes into the room. I look at the form.

Have you ever been injected with high contrast dye?

No.

Do you have any allergies? If so, describe your reaction.

No.

Are you pregnant?

No.

The hallway is empty, but I can hear wind blowing outside. I am surprised that in this big hospital I can hear the wind. There are water stains on the ceiling.

Marjorie's cheerful voice is loud now as she moves to the door. "If you have any cramping, just take a Tylenol." The woman before me emerges in her hospital gown and robe and walks uncomfortably down the hall. I want to ask her what it felt like. But more than that I want to ask her if they found anything. But she does not look at me. There is no shared knowing here, no silent sisterhood. Marjorie calls my name.

The room is much bigger than I expected. It feels too spacious a place to look at these tiny, intimate parts of my body. In the middle is a bed enveloped in buttons and screens. The long thick neck of the HSG machine wraps around it, a giant round head hovering above the empty sheet where I will lie.

The doctor comes in and introduces himself, but his name doesn't settle in my brain. He explains the procedure again. Warning signs of an infection, no intercourse for two days, there may be light spotting and that's normal. "It's a routine test, I do them all the time." There is no irony in this statement, as if routine is transferable. Every day he tells women they have cysts blocking their tubes or fibroids choking their wombs.

He asks me to describe my last period. "I'm going to get you to take a pregnancy test, just to make sure," he says.

Marjorie passes me a cup and leads me out through a different door, where there are more people, another waiting room. I see the daughter from the first waiting room, waiting for her mother with a magazine. Marjorie points to the bathroom. I fill the cup, and I don't know if I should leave it there or bring it back to her. I decide to take it with me, out past the woman with the magazine, holding the warm cup of urine in my hand close against my body. I find Marjorie and pass her my pee.

"Oh, thank you so much!" she says cheerfully. I am not sure if she is sincere or trying to make a joke. "You can go back in and have a seat."

I fantasize that she will return and tell me it's positive. I am amazed, crying with joy and laughter, Marjorie laughing too as she congratulates me. "On the day I found out you were coming," I am telling the young person watching me with her father's eyes, "I was about to have this test." Marjorie returns. She pauses, and sighs.

"Negative," she says sympathetically.

"That's what I expected."

She tells me to take off my robe and underwear, and leads me over to the table. She pats the cushion. "Your head goes here, bum over the hole," she says, and points to a toilet-shaped cushion on the other end of the table. She guides my head down past the round head of the machine. "Watch your head—you're my last patient of the day, I don't have time to do a CT scan for a concussion too!" I force a laugh as she pulls up my gown and drapes the rest of my body with lead sheets. The doctor comes in and Marjorie bustles around him with the bottle of dye. I stare up into the machine's blank round face.

"First I'm going to clean the outside of your vagina," the doctor explains. "Then I'll put in the speculum to expose your cervix. I'll clean that too, and then I'll put in the catheter which will inject the dye."

The leviathan slowly moves down to hover over my pelvis, revealing the ceiling behind it. There, someone has taped a dozen photographs of babies.

One is being held in an exhausted but proud mother's arms, but the rest are detached from their caregivers. Anyone's baby. They lie on their backs in cribs, or on the white sheet of a photographer's studio, dressed up in tiny plaid shirts or onesies with cute sayings. Too small to resemble anyone. Whose babies are these, I want to know. Have these pictures been sent here by mothers who also once lay on this table? Or are they random children meant to remind me of my goal, as the doctor prods at me, poking the catheter into my cervix with a slice of pain? Anyone's baby, maybe yours. I tell myself that they are meant to be inspiring, comforting. But they seem impossibly cruel, hovering up there on the ceiling.

Marjorie moves the machine, snaps a picture. I feel my uterus making a fist around the catheter. Marjorie must have had to stand on the table to place the photos up there, steadying herself against the hysterosalpingogram machine.

"You're done," the doctor says. "And everything looks normal."

"Thank you." I find myself choking on the words. He is still talking.

"I still need to take a closer look at the pictures, but the dye went right through the fallopian tubes, and everything looks clear and healthy."

He breezes out of the room, and I try not to show my eyes welling up as Marjorie lowers the table.

"See, the worst part is the waiting."

"The worst part is the pain," I say. And I hope she thinks that that is what the tears are for.

"Well, you handled it like a trooper!"

She helps me to my feet and hands me washcloths and a giant maxi pad. "We only use a couple tablespoons of dye, but what goes in must come out!" I am nodding, not really listening, wrapping the robe back around myself, doing up my shoes. She is showing me the catheter now. "See, this tiny thing goes in, then this donut part keeps the dye from coming back out." She loves her job, it amazes her. "The fallopian tubes are only the width of a hair."

I feel shaky as I walk back to the change room, wondering if I am dripping blue across the floor. I don't even know what color the dye is, but I picture it the same as the light blue liquid they pour on maxi pads in commercials. Something inoffensive, non-biological. In the change room I wipe myself off and slip back into my clothes, then wander out into the street to phone my husband.

"I'm done, and everything looks normal."

"I knew it would be. How do you feel?"

"Not too bad, a little uncomfortable. A little emotional."

"Good emotional or bad emotional?"

"Good."

And in that moment I think I mean it. But as I hang up I wonder if this is true. Because if the doctor had found something wrong, maybe he would have also found something to fix.

I wonder how old those babies are now, the ones on the ceiling. Do they change the batch every few months, or have the same ones been up there for years, staying two hours, two days, two months old? Looking down on the table at hundreds of women, at diagnoses inconclusive and devastating, at hundreds of private fears, hundreds of lonely griefs. Witnesses, or taunts, or promises. Hidden and then revealed as if from behind a curtain, saying, we have been here all along. We are waiting.

Peonies

Mom says I can take two of the peony bushes from the garden, if I don't leave a bald patch in the bed. I wrote my first poems in the timbre of their perfume. I try to dig up one of each colour. Autumn green, we must guess, the memory of their blooms already blurred into feeling instead of scene.

She always said she had a brown thumb. Yet she gives me a dieffenbachia that was a gift when I was born. Throughout my childhood it stood in the south window and grew, leaning into light, matching my height through the years.

Other things, too, she gives me now. Chafing dishes, mason jars, a bin of tissue paper like pressed leaves. She has no more need for these things, these rooms. She can no longer walk in the yard, she should no longer climb the stairs.

*

In my apartment in Vancouver, I had a pothos plant on the mantle. Pothos are resilient plants, surviving without direct sunlight, bouncing back when unwatered for weeks, perfect for my own brown thumb. Yet when, year after year, I was not pregnant, then was, and then was not again, I examined the plant every day. That tendril was a little longer, that folded leaf was new. We would try an intrauterine insemination, and between the shots of hormone I would track the progress of this little life in my living room like a prayer. And when we moved home to Alberta, to be close to the people we still hoped would someday be grandparents to our children, we would bring the pothos in an orange crate on the backseat.

*

I help her pack the daily dishes, the pictures in their frames. My mother holds the watering can with two frail hands; her brown thumb trembles like a naked branch. She asks me not to walk on carpet vacuumed backwards for new owners. But I take two giant steps across my old room, to the window where I perched my chin when I couldn't sleep.

In case of fire, I planned to follow the ledge to my parents' room, to save them, before we all leapt off the garage. I taste the dusty metal of the screen and think of winter as a verb: trees squirreling their chlorophyll, naked spines of geranium in basement boxes.

*

I plant the peonies beneath my unborn baby's window, reaching past my belly for the hole. Next summer, if they take, their colours will surprise me one morning: pink like an infant's tongue, white like a bone.

Sunday dinners, now, will be at my house, on my dishes. Mom can no longer lift a pot; she should no longer hold a knife. That poor dieffenbachia, she says, seeing it stoop in the corner of my dining room. She sees the stick, so like her own, failing to hold it up. But at the top, pale new leaves are grasping at the winter sun.

On Waiting

I read somewhere that I should walk. So Kent and I walk around the mall among frazzled Christmas shoppers, Boney M thudding under cries of kids queued for Santa and the shuffle of Ugged feet. There is little advice on how to wait, only how to shorten the time. So I eat spicy food, bounce on a yoga ball, rub my own nipples. My belly is striped with angry purple marks, like those of a castaway marking days on a cave wall. Only it is me who is lost, not the child inside, three days overdue. I am stranded in the unknown: the fingers yet uncounted, the skull uninspected, the cry unheard.

*

In university I "waited tables." That phrase is left over from servants who waited in corners for their lords to finish politely masticating. But there was little waiting in my work. Nightmares still, years later, of forgetting a table amidst the rush of WHAT'S ON TAP, NO MAYO, SHARP KNIFE, MORE NAPKINS *KETCHUP* REFILL ORDER UP! ORDER UP! Whatever waiting there was came in moments—for the woman to lean back in her seat so I could set the plate down, for the fountain cola to fill the mug, for the man to lean back so I could take his plate away.

But there is intimacy in this form of waiting. Lifting the napkin crumpled across the top, smeared with lipstick and gravy, revealing the fork shined by the inside of a stranger's mouth, the onions picked out and politely piled. The abandoned burger, cross-sectioned, exposing the contour of the jaw, where teeth sheared bun and meat before lips flipped down over tongue's private work.

*

Sometime in the last month the baby has turned his head down toward my pelvis, slowly readying to enter the world. For weeks, he has hung upside down, unbothered by gravity. Floating in amniotic fluid, fetuses circulate less blood than they will once they are born, through much smaller bodies. Their heads do not rush.

*

Once, I waited for a train to depart for Toronto. The car softly buzzed with a distant iPod, passengers pressed mouths closed around private thoughts, adjusted jackets, and a man boarded with a newspaper under his chin, catching the blood pouring from his face.

The blood ran down the paper crease and his forearms. Several strangers rushed forward with tissues, to hold his glasses, to put a hand on his back, unafraid of the liquid flowing to the carpet. "I tripped—" he said to the car, or to himself, "the stairs—didn't even know I was bleeding." He looked around, a little bewildered, and tried to step off. But the attendant said that he couldn't leave the train until EMS arrived, and therefore the train couldn't leave, either. Policy. He could faint on the platform, even if the bleeding had stopped, even if he sat on that bench, right there. But the bystanders didn't grumble or make agitated calls, they made jokes.

"You have given yourself a nice makeover!"

"Yeah, the nose job is an improvement!"

Slowly the strangers sat down where they had stood, close, twisting out of rows with feet in the aisle or leaning over seat backs, talking somehow about Scotland. I listened from the other end of the car as they slipped off their silence like pinching shoes, made the car their living room.

After an hour, someone from another car came forward to complain to the attendant. From my seat his irritation seemed boorish. But he hadn't seen the red-soaked newspaper, the strangers' tenderness. He hadn't felt the train settle into stillness like relief.

*

Every winter I wait for spring, until finally the sand that was spread on icy roads crusts the last drifts of snow and fills the gutters with gritty mud. The grass revealed in patches is brown and mouldy. It will be months yet, before the first buds appear on the trees. But the first Saturday above 10°, when the sun is strong, people stroll down Whyte Avenue, peeling off coats and tying them around waists. Our bare skin feels tender in the cool air, and we stop for beers on patios and smile at strangers passing by with the shared knowledge of what we have endured. Summer will come. It is more faith than patience. By July we will squander warm days on movies in dark theatres, but for now these days are pale, delicate things, translucent larvae that must be gently cupped.

*

Between my hip bones the resistance of the baby's weight: water pail, milk jug, paper ream. This is the lightest he will ever be.

Once, I waited for Misoprostol to find its way to this place in my body, to shed the tiny bud that had already died there. I wrapped myself in blankets and watched whatever movie was on TV, as the stuff shuddered out, clots disguising placenta and amniotic dribbles, unseen ring of pale spine, no bigger than a grain of rice. It hurt. These are contractions, I realized. I am in labour. But there was relief in pain and gore to match the severity of the wound, this grisly expression of a loss that had been physically invisible. My child.

When the blood was still rushing in the middle of the night, I woke Kent. But as I waited in emerg, the bleeding began to slow on its own. They checked my hemoglobin, which was fine. "Go home and sleep," the gynecology resident said. So I did.

When I didn't have my body to focus on anymore, I began to focus on my mind, and it was then that the reality of what had happened began to sink in. The nature of my wait changed, became waiting until it was possible to try again. If I could replace the baby I had lost, I thought, I could skip this grieving; I could skip this pain.

I went for a lab test every week to make sure that my hormone levels were dropping. My blood still thought I was pregnant, though a little less each time, my body finally seeing the truth, letting go. Yet more than a month later, I was still bleeding and spotting. My brain wanted to move on but my body wouldn't let me. I returned to the same ultrasound clinic where I had found out there was no heartbeat, to sit in the waiting room with happy parents-to-be. The ultrasound showed a tiny piece of the pregnancy remained in me, less than a centimeter long. "Remainders that small are nothing to worry about," my doctor said. "Wait for it to come out on its own. Your next period might be a bit heavier than usual."

A week later I found myself back at emerg, haemorrhaging again. The doctor blurred, receded to the end of a dark hallway, saying "emergency D&C." I was terrified that they would damage my uterus, that they wouldn't be able to stop the bleeding and I would wake up without a womb. Kent tried to make jokes and held my hand; he was terrified that I would die.

After the surgery they said they couldn't believe something so small had caused so much bleeding. A tiny piece left behind, like a hair in a sink. "Wait," it said. "This is not yet over. It will not be so easy to move on."

We went back to work, back to our routines. We went with friends to try the new hipster mac n' cheese place in Kerrisdale. I wanted to talk about what I had gone through. But I didn't know how to bring it up. There were no bandages or slings to start the conversation. So I blurted, fumbling with a pill bottle, "I have to take iron because I haemorrhaged after a miscarriage last week."

"Oh, god, are you okay?"

I nodded, immediately wishing I could take the sentence back. Even wearing those words like a fetid cast, the meaning was faint. They couldn't know, any more than the strangers at the other tables, who saw me waiting just for food.

*

Thirty-eight weeks ago I waited on the phone while a nurse checked the results of my blood test. It was my third intrauterine insemination, a step before IVF in which hormone injections supercharge the ovaries and the sperm is inserted directly into the cervix by syringe. The first of these had ended in another miscarriage the year before, followed by another haemorrhage and another emergency D&C. Every month between and since, the bleeding was a renewal of that grief. Not because it was a reminder, but because it was the same.

"Congratulations!" the nurse said in my ear. "You are pregnant!" As I processed these words my body did not feel any different. Again and again it held secrets from myself, like a stranger, just as my own future is a secret from myself.

Now, I have a habit of caressing my own belly, as if it is this new child's skin, already outside of me. I share with him my food, the shelter of my body, and he shares his hiccups, his waste. But even when he is born, I won't yet know the colour of his eyes.

Maybe some night I will wait for him in the kitchen, an hour or two past his curfew, with visions of twisted metal and clothes smeared with blood. He will enter, safe, using his hood to hide the blush of booze, of having toed the threshold of virginity. "Where have you been?" I'll squawk, which is to say, *I was so worried.*

Right now, my child is the closest to me he will ever be. But still hiding his face, his body, using my own blood and skin. I count the minutes between kicks, poke the firm places hinting knee or skull to make him wake and move. And I know now that I was wrong—the grief doesn't leave. The fear doesn't leave. It will wait me out.

It's late, my child, so late. Where have you been?

In Pleasantview Cemetery

My child does not sleep, so I go walking among the bones of the dead. The stroller wheels click along the path, trees frame panes of light across the rows. Beneath simple verses are the plots, green and even as the shelves of a library.

Granite markers shine like kitchen counters. There is love here. And flowers. Their names: Sandrich, Nguyen, Bukowski. Their dates cup like hands around a moth, a life fluttering, hidden within. What will the dash contain for this child, cooing in his stroller, fighting sleep with tiny fists? What would my mother say the dash has held for her, as she nears the end of her too short life?

They live on in our hearts, and will forever. Roses for love, orb for faith. A broken branch for a life cut short. I begin to see only names that are English words: Cook. Priest. Silk. Hall. Hull. Young. Yet those who left these flowers know their histories. Homelands left. New loves, tender, larval. The birth of children. Scars of labours. Long winters of loss.

Is it disrespectful, then, to stroll here, to see in these stones a symbol of a thing, an apron splattered with grease, a stiff collar? Hall: a long corridor. Young: a child in blue sleepers, kicking, looking, awake.

There is too much in the world to miss behind closed eyes. The way the aspen leaves jangle like green coins. The ant bearing a beetle on its back. Everything with wheels: bicycle, car, garbage truck. How a bud begins, pale and smooth as an eyelid.

What will the dash contain, for he who is just beginning?

Hull: the rough hewn boat.

Silk: the worm's breath of thread.

Home

As I pass the lounge to my mother's room, the woman on TV is showing how to make meringue. White and peaked like the heads above the wheelchairs, parked in a row. Everything here is sweet, Mom says, even the waxed beans, plopped from a can. The pork chop.

I bring her fresh pineapple—fruit not tinned with maraschino cherries, catatonic mandarins. These offerings are my small recompense.

She does not want to be here. She is a generation younger than almost all the other residents on her floor, whose minds all seem tuned to a different channel. "Ah do," one of them says over and over, "ah do." My mother tells me it's all she ever says.

We call it "the home," cruel euphemism for white linoleum and vinyl armchairs, call buttons on hospital beds. Yet this is where she keeps her toothbrush, her clothes, the photos of her family. This is where she sleeps and eats—or pushes plates away. This is where she writes. No longer plays, but poems, character sketches of the people she lives with.

This lady wears all her clothes at once, one on top of the other... Florence is the one you hear crying out "I'm lost."

*

My parents still have the same conversation they had for months—years—before she moved here. Why can't she live at home with him? Because he can't take care of her himself. It is a conversation made possible only by their privilege; the costs of different care options are all extraordinary.

I have been drawn into the middle of these conversations again and again, each one a fish full of bones I must carefully pull from my mouth. She hates it here—couldn't they hire more home care?...He doesn't think the home care nurses were reliable, and what if they called in sick again?...These are the last months of her life... Her condition will only worsen; there are pills in the night, sometimes oxygen, he still has to work... She has no one to talk to... And what if she falls?

I want to advocate for her, and I want her to be safe, and I want my father to have enough reserves for love as well as care. You don't really know, they both say.

She writes a poem about Dad and his new bike, imagining him dashing through the river valley, free of her illness and this place. She wants to go home; she wants to ride with him along the trails, feeling the breeze on her face.

No one has ever suggested I take on her care. I am eight months pregnant and the mother of a toddler, I have a job. But my shameful secret is how relieved I feel not to be considered for that role. I don't feel equipped for the physical intimacy, the viscera of this labour. Caring for my child is different. There is no history before his need. My mother and I have gone through the process of growing apart as I grew up, of becoming separate. Her body, once my home, is now her private dwelling.

Across her doorway my dad has strung a bright yellow NO ENTRY tape, to keep out the wandering man. But the nurse enters unceremoniously, with pills in a tiny cup of yogurt. She doesn't know that in her head my mother is writing a poem about her.

She dabs, and dots, she wipes and smears.
She thinks she's doing you a favour.
No one would guess you want to lick your own lips.

*

"Home again, home again, lickety-split," she'd say as we turned in the driveway, no matter how far away we'd been, how long the journey. She lived for thirty years in that house, in that kitchen. She had embraced the labour of homemaking by alternating between the mushroom soup casseroles of the eighties and panko-crusted dishes pulled from *Gourmet* magazine. She considered colour on the plate. In this work she both nourished her family and nourished herself. This was the centre of my childhood home; an elaborate meal served to the sound of the six o'clock news, always with something green.

But that's not where she wants to go now. Three years ago, she and Dad moved to a highrise condo overlooking a bustling street, the river beyond. She had dreamed of moving for years, away from the looming transmission towers and long, lonely driveways of suburbia to the life of downtown. When she got sick, the move became a necessity as much as a wish. But she thought she'd at least be able to stay at that window as the disease progressed, looking down at the traffic, at the speed of other lives.

The nurse asks if she will come out for dinner tonight. She declines politely. Dad will be here later, with a Tupperware of supper he has made from one of her recipes. He never used to cook; he lumbers through this clinically, considering what she can chew.

She used to eat with all the power of her small body. She once broke a molar on an olive, biting down too hard on a hidden pit. A crunchy carrot would echo across the room with elegant conviction. Now she chews slowly, labours to swallow, opening her mouth for Dad to put the next forkful in. And it is in the space between that she seems most vulnerable, her lips apart, waiting for the food. So she will advise him, too much salt, or not enough.

*

The people who bought my family's old house have torn it down and built something new there. I am not affected by this news. The building had ceased to be mine when my parents moved their possessions, when my family transitioned from being cared for by my mother to managing her care. Home, in the sense of the place of childhood, was already a memory to which I could not return.

*

I help Mom position M on her lap with one of the books he brought. Her reading is slow, slurred, but she intones as the actress she once was; she does not stumble over the rhythm of the poetry. As she read to me in bed when I was small. Back then, when my parents talked about home, they were referring to Newfoundland, where they were born and met as teenagers. They were twenty-three when Dad brought Mom here to Edmonton, knowing no one. This was how I first learned how home could split, multiply, become variously an origin, a kitchen, another person.

M slumps, getting comfortable, oblivious to his own weight. He seems so big on her, his body pulling her down into the upholstery on one side, his chubby legs sticking out into the room. She must feel bony, like a plastic toy left on the chair. But he is ignorant of her disease; he doesn't wonder why she's here. Sometimes, he gets a sticker when I'm signing the visitor registration. When speaking to him, we call this "Nanny's place."

I know it is unlikely he will remember this, remember her, when she is gone. Just as I don't remember the grandfather who died when I was four. All of my grandparents were in St. John's, over 4000 kilometres away, when long distance calls cost too much to waste on kids. I still felt their love, somehow, from sporadic visits and birthday cards; it was tied up in that word my parents used—home—along with Purity brand crackers and ocean and fiddle music, the exotic and the familiar, and a feeling that was like both wishing and losing.

But Newfoundland is not where my mother wants to go, either. She is not nostalgic. She is focused now on daily needs, on managing pain, on how to live as she approaches the end of her life. She wants to go somewhere of her own making.

*

When M was about to be born, Mom told the story, again, of my own birth. How her parents had been visiting from Newfoundland to meet me, but I was two weeks late and they were about to fly back. How during a checkup the obstetrician reached into her and broke her water without warning, saying, "We can't have any disappointed grandparents, now, can we?" This is the crux of the story, what is so clearly now a misogynist, violent act but was just accepted in 1979. But this is not the end of my birth story, for after the labour, the delivery, the first suckles and the stitches, there is a new child and a new mother who must reconstruct her life and body around this being. My mother was nursing me, rocking me; it was the middle of the night, and I wouldn't stop crying. She wondered why her own mother didn't come to help her. The next morning, when my mother asked, my grandmother said tenderly, "it was your first night with your new baby. I didn't want to intrude." My mother has carried this moment like a little scar, recounted it as if still trying to convince herself of its wisdom. Her mother went back to Newfoundland; my dad worked endless shifts as a medical resident; she was alone with me.

I can see them, the mother cradling the infant, straddling the sacred and the profane, the beginning of a never ending grasping at and misunderstanding of need.

*

My grandmother passed away in a place like this. At the end of her life, she was almost completely deaf and lost in dementia. My mother used scrap paper to ask her questions, as if both trying to communicate and trying to test her cognitive function.

What's your name?
Nellie Mary Noseworthy, 88 Berteau Avenue
What's my name?
Elizabeth.

Reading these notes now I can trace a kind of conversation, see where Nanny scrawled something sort of legible, guess where she must have answered aloud.

Where is Jean?
...Where is home?

An address, a table, a place where we are cared for.

*

We call this facility "the home." Yet in this room I don't know if I should wear my shoes or take them off. In this room I don't know where to sit, or what to say. I don't know if I should help her myself when she needs to use the bathroom, or call the nurse. I know she will say to call the nurse. I want to call the nurse. I am afraid of doing things wrong, of hurting her, of dropping her. I am afraid of entering the shadows—seeing the folds of her aged body, the diaper. Of breaching her privacy and my sovereignty. I am afraid of knowing things I won't forget, of seeing into unwanted futures.

She points to her top dresser drawer, where she keeps a stash of dark expensive chocolate. One with sea salt, one with orange, shiny paper declaring cocoa in percentages. I break off squares, we sample and compare, we share the bitterness.

She hates the sleeping old women dreaming of the lemon pies of their youth, hates the sweet mushy food, the apparatus of bars and buttons around the toilet. She hates this body, its trembling, its pain, its betrayal. She wants a solid floor and a warm kitchen for her homeless mind.

And when I get up and walk away from here, I feel like I'm taking it from her. My able feet, my working tongue. My belly, heavy and stretched, engrossed with beginnings.

My mother feels she doesn't belong here because she is so much younger than everyone else. But in truth, no one belongs here, no matter how old, how confused. Not everyone can live in a house or with a loved one, but everyone should have dignity and autonomy. Everyone should feel at home in the place where they sleep.

*

I hug her goodbye, tell her I will call her tomorrow. In the hall the old people are gathering for dinner. The TV blares on. Fine granulated sugar will dissolve best. Slowly add it to the egg whites. They will begin to take on a glossiness, then to form soft peaks. Continue to beat until the peaks are stiff, when the whites reach up after the beaters, as if to say, stay. As if to say, please don't go.

A, B, O

It always seemed like the third blood type should be C. Alphabet of our survival, elements of every word and every being. How blood flows to clean a wound, clotting to close it. How it flows to loose spent eggs and builds again to nest them. Carrier of my ancestors' codes, flowing through my mother, through me, through my daughter. And now, in the minutes after her birth, pooling between the tissues of my womb. As if there is too much to say for our bodies to hold it.

This is what my maternal body does. When my first child was born, I bled too much. Just as I bled too much when other lives let go. Haemorrhages of words, floods of O, O, O.

In her final months my post-menopausal mother has also begun to bleed again, her broken brain searching any channel to new life. O Mom, you are watching from your wheelchair in the corner of the room, *Do not resuscitate unless my granddaughter has not yet been born*. You have been waiting for this day, for her birth, to begin your own death.

Instead, you may be watching mine. It began in the hour after the baby's first suckle, pain and fear trying to match the intensity of joy. The nurses don't believe me, but you see it, hear me say, worse than birth. Watch my baby's father scoop her up off my bed as I writhe, watch him search for someone who will help me, shouting in the nurse's station. Until finally a doctor hailed down in the hall sees me, says the words, *O.R. Massive hematoma*. Balloon of blood, another child's worth within the walls. Between tissues meant to rest against each other like the pages of a book.

*

We talk about birth and death as being intertwined but opposite, like an entrance and an exit through the same door. How close giving birth brings us to that threshold, both in the physiological danger that stills hangs over it, and in the philosophical and existential questions that surround it—how the next generation forces us to contemplate the end of our own, how in giving birth we have started a clock that is already counting down for an unknown time to our child's own death.

And yet. What if instead of the door, the entrance and exit, a birth begins with A. Or B, or any combination of twenty-six letters, signifying sounds, then meaning, beginning stories. What if we begin *in medias res*, protagonists to our own stories but inseparable from the worlds made before us, the patterns we hold in our bodies?

And if this is birth, then death is not the opposite, but the echo of a telling in the silence after it, the words recalled on the scent of a soap, in the heat of summer. The prequel to countless other tales begun in blood or in our movements through a scene.

*

When I awake after the surgery, my daughter is waiting, washed and swaddled, wearing a tiny white toque. Eager to nurse, her mouth an O around my nipple. Ignorant of where her mother has been, just as I, under anaesthetic, have been ignorant to these first moments of her care. My story, now, will always have her at its centre. But her story, just beginning, is already diverging.

O Mom. I have survived to be mother to this child, and you will live a few more months, to be mine. But the book always opens on its own, asking to be read again. The book is always being written: A, B, O.

III. Apple, Earth

micrographia micrographia micrographia micrographia micrographia micrographia micrographia micrographia micrographia jennifer bowering delisle micrographia micrographia micrographia

Passage

My mother has chosen November 28th as the day that she will die. It will be in the den of my parents' condo, overlooking the river. She wants my brother and me at either hand, my husband at her feet, my father at her head. She has asked us to sing to her.

We have two weeks, then, to say goodbye. In some ways we have been saying goodbye for years, as we have watched her limbs lock, her head become too heavy for her neck, her voice disappear into her chest. Her passing has been on a schooner without wind, her body slowly getting smaller, still waving from the deck. But now the timeline is set, we can count down her life in hours. And I must still unload the dishwasher, and get my children dressed, and buy milk.

Five months ago, Bill C-14 was passed in Parliament, to legalize and regulate medical assistance in dying. She considers herself lucky, to have this process open to her now, that she doesn't have to go to Quebec or Switzerland, that she doesn't have to find a way to do it illegally, or wait in pain and fear until her body lets her go.

*

Whereas the Parliament of Canada recognizes the autonomy of persons who have a grievous and irremediable medical condition that causes them enduring and intolerable suffering and who wish to seek medical assistance in dying;

*

I can't visit her in the long-term care home this week because my children have a cold. We FaceTime every day, and she watches the baby suck on her fingers, and my son would rather play with his trucks. And I don't know what to talk about. There must be things that I will wish I had asked her. Details about my childhood milestones, stories from her own past, who crocheted that, who is in this photograph. I can only think to talk about who visited today, and how she is feeling. I have to ask her to repeat each answer two or three times before I can discern the words inside the mumbling of her lips. I keep telling her, "I'm sorry, I didn't get that. I'm sorry."

When I was in school, "euthanasia" was a topic in debate club. We watched Sue Rodriguez in her wheelchair on the 6 o'clock news, head propped with a towel, and argued whether she had the right to die on her own terms. *Euthanasia*: a good death. Thanatos, twin of Sleep, wingèd boy, gently carries the fallen to Elysium. *What's wrong with youth-in-Asia? Hahaha.*

Until 2015, it was a form of "culpable homicide" in the *Criminal Code*. The Supreme Court of Canada ruled that this prohibition was a violation of Section 7 of the Charter of Rights and Freedoms: "Section 7 is rooted in a profound respect for the value of human life. But s. 7 also encompasses life, liberty and security of the person during the passage to death." This word "passage" makes me think of steerage—dark, rat-infested holds.

To access the Medical Assistance in Dying program, or MAiD, her disease must cause intolerable physical or psychological suffering. She must be in an advanced state of irreversible decline. Her natural death must be reasonably foreseeable. In the presence of two witnesses, my mother signed and dated a statement that she wishes to die. She was informed about the other means available to relieve her suffering, and told that she may withdraw her consent at any time. Now she must wait at least ten days. She will confirm her consent again immediately before the procedure.

In the meantime, I am writing her obituary. We are devastated to announce the passing of Elizabeth Bowering, age 62, on a date that has not yet come. And the devastation has not yet come. I have to assume that this is what will eventually replace the numbness, the robotic execution of daily duties. The milk will last longer than she will.

*

Whereas robust safeguards, reflecting the irrevocable nature of ending a life, are essential to prevent errors and abuse in the provision of medical assistance in dying;

*

Thanatos is often depicted holding a butterfly in one hand, to represent the soul no longer tethered by the human body, its oppressive gravity. In the other, he usually holds an inverted torch, for the life gone out. He is the son of Nyx and Erebos, of Night and Darkness.

*

She doesn't want a traditional funeral. She wants a party, with wine and laughter. I like this idea, of remembering her with joy. But I don't know where mourning fits in to this plan. My dad is looking at venues, emailing me reception menus. The Light Grazing package. The Satisfying package. The Fulfilling package. If we do it in December, this one will be decorated for Christmas.

My dad and I share the same defence mechanism of focusing on logistical details. But my subconscious has realized what's going on, creating not an acute, palpable grief but a kind of ambient sadness. I watch legal dramas and shop for new towels online.

What does one wear to a death?

A friend asks me if I am angry with my mother. It hadn't occurred to me that this could be a legitimate way to feel. Mom can hardly bear the pain in all her joints. On several mornings she has awakened long before her body, unable to move. Disabled lives are worth living—but my mother can see her worsening symptoms, her approaching death, and says she is sure of her choice. Every moment with her grandchildren is precious, but also a reminder that no matter how long she can hold on, she still will not see my son read, my daughter walk. The baby shoves a toy in her mouth, and Mom succumbs to sobs that shake her whole body, leave her gasping. I wipe her nose.

*

Whereas it is important to affirm the inherent and equal value of every person's life and to avoid encouraging negative perceptions of the quality of life of persons who are elderly, ill or disabled;

*

When we arrive today, Mom's friend Judy is already there. Judy holds the baby and chats about her own grandchildren, and how long it takes to get to the home on the new ring road. I take the children for a walk in the hallway while Judy and my mother say their last goodbye.

I have to keep M from climbing on the electric wheelchair, playing with the oxygen machine, and pressing the giant red call button. So I put *PAW Patrol* on the TV and let him sit on her bed while I nurse the baby, making a weak joke about it screwing up her Netflix suggestions. This week in preschool he is learning about dinosaurs. I am trying to explain that dinosaurs do not live anymore, that they are gone. Mom teaches him the word "extinct." But he thinks she means stinky, and laughs.

When she first got her wheelchair, he was 18 months old. He pointed to it and said "tractor." We called it "Nanny's tractor" after that. He hasn't known her without her disease, has never seen her run, or even walk unaided. Has never heard her sing the way she did when I was growing up, powerful but controlled vibrato, always as if she were on stage. Because she needs a straw for her water, he gets one too. If he wonders why she cannot pick him up, or why my dad feeds her at Sunday supper, he has not asked. He does not need a word for her condition, only for her vehicles. But what do I tell him, now? Two weeks from now? How will I explain "dead," when I can't point to it, when he can't touch it, or hear it, or put it in his mouth? How will I explain something I can barely understand myself?

*

Whereas vulnerable persons must be protected from being induced, in moments of weakness, to end their lives;

*

Elysium is at the western edge of the Earth, where it never snows or even rains. The blessed dead never toil; they wear garlands of flowers and are caressed by ocean breezes. In early Greek mythology, the Elysian Fields are reserved for those related to the gods, but the concept evolved over the centuries to include the righteous and heroic. As paradise became accessible to mortals, the image of Thanatos changed too, from a fierce and bearded brute to a nubile beauty whose cold smooth arms bear the dead on their passage from the cruel world to the afterlife.

*

I suggest to M that he draw Nanny a picture. He is practicing his circles, creating creatures with giant eyes and long trailing lines he says are fingers. On purple construction paper he draws a blob he tells me is Nanny dressed as Spiderman.

The procedure will only take a few minutes. First, the doctor will give her an anti-anxiety drug, then a coma-inducing agent, then finally the neuromuscular blocker that will stop her breath. The date is set but not the time. My mother suggests 2 o'clock. Dad asks, so, do you want to have lunch? Mom begins to giggle. And we all begin to giggle.

There are models everywhere for how to be in the days before a loved one's death. We gather at her bedside in her hospital room, sleeping in chairs, taking turns to run home and shower, until the machine beeps, we shout for the doctor, but she has slipped away. But there are no movie scenes for this kind of waiting. My dad is taking her back to the condo for the last three days of her life, and my aunt is flying in to help him take care of her. I have to wait to go over until they are back from getting groceries.

*

Whereas suicide is a significant public health issue that can have lasting and harmful effects on individuals, families and communities;

*

We spend the morning prepping food to take to the condo for her last supper. We suggested a smorgasbord of some favourite dishes. She chose cod au gratin, a dish that reminds her of her Newfoundland birthplace and a perennial Sunday dinner when I was growing up. Greek chicken marinated in yogurt. Roasted potatoes, chocolate mousse with Grand Marnier. They are things that she loves but also things that she can still chew and swallow with less difficulty. They are things that she made herself when she could still stand at the stove, still bring the spoon to her mouth to check the seasoning.

She has received emails from dozens of people. My aunt and I help her reply, reusing the carefully crafted phrases she has whispered to us. She must comfort them now, tell them that she has had a good life, that she is at peace. It must seem to many that this way of exiting the world is exemplary of "acceptance." But while my mother is eager for the relief of death, she is not ready for the end of her life. She told me not long after she got sick that she did not believe in Heaven. Any remaining embers of her casual Christianity were snuffed out by her diagnosis. But it is not fear of the "undiscovered country" that makes her body tremble now. My mother has been to the islands in the west of Greece, that model for Elysium, and drank wine and eaten grilled fish and been caressed by the ocean's breezes. She wants to stay in *this* world, to make art and make supper and make jokes with her children, go to the theatre, and see her grandchildren grow up alongside the high school sweetheart she has stayed with for forty years.

The Supreme Court's decision to overturn the prohibition of medical assistance in dying is based on the truth that for the patient, "this is a decision that is rooted in their control over their bodily integrity; it represents their deeply personal response to serious pain and suffering. By denying them the opportunity to make that choice, the prohibition impinges on their liberty and security of the person." My mother has chosen to have her brother speak at her memorial, to have Eva Cassidy's "Somewhere Over the Rainbow" played. She has chosen to give her friend a favourite blue scarf. She has chosen to take her final breaths in a room with a view of the river. She is not choosing between living and dying, but between degrees of suffering. The means of her passage.

Her shrunken stomach is full, and her jaw is tired from chewing. Half of the food remains on her plate. My husband jokingly asks if she wants to save it for tomorrow. "Yes," she says. Then giggles. "I forgot!"

We haven't told my son what is happening. We don't want him to believe that death is always planned, or to put too much pressure on their last goodbye. He gives her a hug, one of us holding him up so he can reach his arms around her neck. We take the elevator down.

*

Whereas, in light of the above considerations, permitting access to medical assistance in dying for competent adults whose deaths are reasonably foreseeable strikes the most appropriate balance...

*

This morning the city is entombed in fog, unusual for Edmonton, as if to remind her of Newfoundland. It fits, this dreariness, but it blocks the view of the city that she imagined as the backdrop to her final breaths. Here on the sixteenth floor, there is nothing beyond the window but pale grey light. On the balcony the patio furniture is shrouded for the winter, like ghosts in the mist.

Sometime in the night my dad and aunt and brother have removed all the furniture from the den. I can see the place through the open French doors, the empty window waiting for her recliner to be moved in from the living room.

The phone rings—the doctor and the nurse are here. The doctor is soft-spoken, calls my mother sweetie, sets up his paperwork on top of the piano. "There is no timeline," he says, "take as much time as you need." He hangs back, like a bad odour in the room, impossible to ignore. My mother doesn't want to wait, doesn't want to milk every second from her last morning. "Let's get this over with," she whispers.

"Sorry Mom?"

"Let's get this over with."

*

On a recovered column from the ruined temple of Artemis in Ephesos, Thanatos's wings are made of marble. On his damaged chest, the rough texture of exposed stone. His broken knees make it seem like he has been kneeling.

*

Now, therefore, Her Majesty, by and with the advice and consent of the Senate and House of Commons of Canada, enacts as follows:

*

We move her chair into the den. She wants the blanket her cousin crocheted for her on her legs. We spend a few minutes trying to get her comfortable, adjusting the pillows behind her back and her head, reclining her to the best angle. The fog has burned off, and we all say the sun has come out for her. The doctor places forms in front of her, shows her where to sign. Someone guides her hand to the place, and she struggles to make a few scratches until there is enough of a mark of her consent. The nurse is bustling in the background, setting out syringes on a tray. They put in the IV. Mom whispers for someone to sing, and instead of singing I translate for her, repeating the request to my brother.

"I was going to wait until..." he says.

"She wants it now."

His usually strong voice warbles through "Bridge Over Troubled Water," and though I know it, I can't join in. I am looking out the window, I am stroking her hand.

She is sobbing, and the doctor tells her he is going to give her the anti-anxiety drug now, is that okay? She nods. I watch her face as it begins to relax, and then she begins a soft snore. I am still waiting for the doctor to say that he is about to administer the coma drug, but it has already happened. I kiss her, hastily, tell her, "I love you so much Mom." But she is already asleep. Her breath changes to a kind of gasp, then her mouth falls open, and my dad says, "she's gone."

She's already gone.

I'm angry with the doctor for not giving me a warning, for robbing me of her final moment of consciousness. But I had two weeks to say whatever I might have said. The truth is I still don't know what the words would have been. Everything felt too planned, too precise. I didn't want my last words to her to be rehearsed. Instead, I said nothing.

*

After its careful reasoning and laboured warnings, the law is a performative—in stating that medical assistance in dying is legal, it becomes so. We receive the *Act* as action, as we receive the syringe—as citizen, as body, as patient and witness. We are the object, not the subject. Other kinds of language fail in the face of it. Art fails in the face of it.

Whereas there is justice but not fairness, whereas there is release but not comfort. Whereas there is mercy but not liberty.

*

Brute or beauty, Thanatos has quietly scooped my mother up. She is being carried, too soon, on the passage to death she has chosen. We hope gently.

Sparrow

Soft oversized sweatshirt—putting it on the closest thing in years to receiving a hug from my mother. I have given the hugs to her, instead, bent down, all elbows, the wheelchair between us. Trying to comfort her as I comfort my own children. No, not like that—gingerly, slender vase, teacup too full.

Yellow panel skirt, flared like the sun. Her favourite colour—her bridesmaids, her board game piece. Her daughter's room, same lemon as that old gingham bedspread. Clothes younger than her body let her be. The only family photo with my children, deadweight arm yoked across her grandson's shoulders, grimace like the sun that day was too bright.

Boho tunic with bell sleeves, her era in style again, folk songs in coffee shops and hair straightened on an ironing board. When we teach a child size, we show her, little ball, big ball. Your hand, my hand. Not apple, Earth. Not nightlight, sun. Yet, I thought loss was the lesson when she sang "Where Have All the Flowers Gone?" *Gone to soldiers every one.* The kind of loss that fills a field, a generation. *Long time asking,* the song goes, but I thought I understood.

Geometric jersey sundress. Too much her, like trying on her skin.

Black cashmere sweater. Each piece has a label with her name adhered inside, though she wouldn't let the home wash most of them. Delicate cycle, or hand wash, lay flat and reshape. She liked fine things, Burberrys, Laurens. French gel manicures, rack of lamb, Shiraz through a straw in a small child's cup.

Pencil skirts in every colour. How to put on pantyhose: thumbs inside one leg, gather up the nylon into a ring around your toe, then roll it up, coffee mole vanishing into Barbie sheen. Never shave above your knees.

Long black dress for cruise ship dancing, spaghetti straps for tanned skin and touch.

Grey funnel neck with buttons, that she wore the night before she died. Could I wear this, could I wear any of these, to buy honeydew, sniffing the ripe rind?

Deep blue scarf, draping like rain.

Cowl neck blouse, Lycra hoodie, t-shirt in bone. There must have been a time that I was smaller than her, small enough to fit inside the cropped body, the tight arms. But most of these clothes are too small for me. Even when she could still stand, I stood a head taller. Garbage bags fill for the women's shelter, shoe heels and belt prongs poking holes in the plastic.

Slender gloves I pulled on her fingers, the zippers I zipped, the laces I kneeled to tie, as her body shrank, collar bones holding skin like clothespins.

Sparrow wings flitting out of cuffs, reaching up.

"Guitar for Christmas"

This is where the record skips. My small fingers, shiny with butter, press the cutters into dough and the guitar strum stutters. Roll it out again; when it sticks we add more flour; roll forward not down. This is the album my mother loved, I tell my son; these are the shapes we made when I was a girl. Bird, star, crescent moon. I guide his fingers, shiny and small, the song does not skip where my ear expects it to. This is not the old vinyl, not the old laminate tabletop. The skip is missing and you are missing. This bridge, these chords, their resolution an aberration. The missing chords are missing and you have been dead two weeks now. Press the cutters in, bird, crescent moon. Roll forward. Put the sharp side down, this is the shape of the hole. Listen, can you hear it?

Any Resemblance to Actual Persons

"Happy third birthday!" my mother says to my son. "By now, I bet you have perfected your jumping." She recorded these videos with my brother's help, one for each birthday for each child for the next five years. But I am watching alone.

I have not yet shown this to M; I am unsure if I should. She didn't know when she recorded this nearly a year ago that his third birthday would fall just weeks after her death. Yet she knew what age to start with; she knew she would not live out the year.

She sits in the office of my parents' condo, leaning on the desk, wearing a headset to pick up her quiet voice. Every facial expression is deliberate, practiced. She chuckles, telling him that when he first learned to walk, he chased her and her walker around the kitchen island. She tells him about decorating the Christmas tree at her condo last year—she widens her eyes—"we knew you were helping because all the decorations were hung at the same kid-height!"

I asked her to make the videos, not realizing how much of a labour it would be for her—planning what to say for each, adjusting to address a growing child she no longer knew, doing take after take because her voice was faltering, her words were slurring.

The birthdays were simply a framing device. I had wanted to take advantage of the time we had left, to preserve something for the children who, in time, would not remember her. A video seemed like it would be a bigger piece of her—her face in motion; her mannerisms, even tremoured by disease; the sound of her voice, even slurred by atrophy.

Instead, it feels like she is wearing a mask of herself.

I saw my mother act in many plays at the community theatre and the Fringe over the years. She was a theatre actor, her gestures and expressions always big enough for the back row. She had a particular voice for the stage, an acting voice, more obvious, perhaps, to me, who knew her ordinary voice and manner so well. This is the voice she uses now—not projecting, but musical in her intonation. She asks him questions, even pausing in case he replies. "Do you know all your numbers and letters?" She pulls up her eyebrows in a question, then carries on, not knowing if he responded or not, smiling as if he did, never to know the answer.

She is here and not here, reading a script from the screen that records her, the high tones and muggy expressions that people use with young children exaggerated by the camera, the distance of time, the barrier of death. Maybe this was a mistake.

"Before your second birthday, you could count to ten...but always left out one number. 1, 2, 3...5, 6, 7..." She is speaking into the microphone, she is looking at the camera. "Do you live in the same house you did when you were two?" she asks, and describes the house to him, stretching her lips around the words. "Do you remember?" But we haven't moved, we're still talking about neighbourhoods, casually checking the listings. She is here and not here, projecting herself into the wrong future.

I have already decided I won't show him the video—it will be confusing, maybe even traumatic. I feel guilty about this, that I am rejecting a gift that I asked for and that she worked so hard on, that I am denying my son this last chat with her. But M is too young to choose for himself, and his well-being is more important to me than anything else.

*

My dad has had my family's old VHS home videos digitized. I watch them with the kids one evening. There I am at four, putting ornaments on a Christmas tree heavy with silver garland. And there is Mom, not yet 30, thick dark hair halfway down her back, trim in a festive red sweater. "Gra-ant," she sings to my brother, fourteen months old, "don't touch it honey." I am amazed as the baby turns and waddles off in a different direction, amazed that she sounds surprised when she laughs, "Grant, don't put it in your mouth!"

It's the same voice as in the video for M, only clearer, lighter. Did she always sound like this when we were tiny, these patient words, perfect elocution, musical tones? I can remember her voice, before it was changed by illness. But I don't remember it before it was changed by my growing up.

Then I catch it, the furtive glance at the camera. She sees the red light. Is she performing here then, too? Whom did she imagine watching these, scrutinizing her? Did she imagine me, sitting with my own children? Did she imagine me mourning her?

The tapes had to be significantly restored just for them to play. Even so, the colours are dull and grainy; occasionally a thick white line squeegees down the screen, like someone is trying unsuccessfully to clear the dinge.

With a small child we are often acting, trying to hide our frustration, our exhaustion, our boredom. With a dying loved one, we act too—finding the line between assuring them that we will be okay and assuring them that they will be missed. The dying one, in turn, acts as if they are not grief-stricken, not terrified. What is it, then, really, that made the birthday video feel so uncanny, even grotesque?

"Do you think these decorations are a little too close together?" she asks me.

"That's okay, it will look nice," answers four-year-old me.

Watching my more recent mother, the mother easier to remember, the mother talking directly to the camera, I did not cry. But I cry at this mother of 1983, so young, unbearably beautiful, a family just birthed, worried about the decorations and the vacuum in the frame, ignorant that in a mere thirty years she would be staring at her own death. There is a relief in these tears, a relief from the uncanny, the ridiculous echoes, snowflake ornaments sharing a branch. I can grieve her here because death is an accident of this genre, not a feature. I know how to read this text.

I am crying for my loss and for hers, for that ignorance, but also for the certainty, for the way that death always haunts us in its possibility, its imminence. I am crying as a daughter and a mother.

*

She is telling him about when he was a baby. "The only way I could hold you," she says, "was if someone put you in my lap." Her tongue sounds thick in her mouth.

She is here and not here, projecting herself into a future that cannot exist.

"These arms have always ached for you, M," she says. "And I hope you know why I couldn't pick you up and swing you around, because I sure wanted to." She is no longer speaking to a three-year-old. That phrasing is for a man who does not yet exist, who will not remember whether he knew why she couldn't pick him up. And it is for me, her poet daughter, trying to make sense of what I am seeing. She chose these words carefully; I can see her reading. Beneath the contrived tones she is trying to say something true.

Maybe this was a mistake not just of genre, but of audience. Of not knowing how to watch, not knowing how to grieve.

We ask our questions, we pause, we carry on.

Birthmark

My father-in-law has a large stain on his forearm—"port-wine," like a glass tipped over. Not wine but Appleton's, diet Pepsi, no ice. We say *birthmark*, as if we are scarred by entering the world. Yet it is more like birth warned of bruises not yet felt—those that would be made by loss, those that would be made by his father.

My daughter has a tiny birthmark in the same place on her forearm. Marker dot, drip of jam. There are more pronounced ways that she resembles her grandfather. But there is something in how the forearm peeks out of folded shirt cuffs, how we hold it against our bodies. The forearm carries the radial and ulnar arteries, those wide channels from the heart, so close to the surface of the skin.

Both their bodies limit speech—her age, Bob's pain. Instead she brings him the stones that his partner collects in little dishes and jars around the house. Red striped agate; turquoise, shaped like a boat. I watch him accept her offerings until the rocks spill onto the carpet, his birthmark matched on the other arm by cancer's purple bruises.

*

Bob was never much for talking, anyway. He would phone to ask about the weather, hanging up when he knew there was snow, and we were well. It would have been easier if I could talk hockey, to fill those silences when Kent left the room. Snow, sun, watching the children busy at their little missions. Yet on every birthday he picked out a card for me himself, one of those in swirly script that called me daughter, and the Hallmark poems seemed like his, and true.

All his life he has figured things out for himself—rebuilding engines, inventing tools out of hockey pucks, parenting, tenderness, love. How to go on when the ones you love have left you behind. Rum without violence. Rarely, if he had enough and they were alone, he would tell Kent or his brother about his own father. I never heard him tell any of these stories. They came to me in fragments, shards that stood for the cut, for the kick.

My daughter points to her own body: eye, nose, belly, elbow, toes. She puts her finger on her dot, presses into it, wondering why it is there, and what it is for. Once, birthmarks were called longing marks, thought to take the shape of what a mother craved in pregnancy. I wonder what Kent's grandmother longed for, as she waited for the birth of her child, the first of seven. The strength of black spruce, stretching its limbs despite the acid of its muskeg ground. A child who would see the pain ahead, marked on his skin like a map, and brace himself for it. A child who would survive his father's hand and the limits of her power to protect him. It is 1963. The boy is fifteen, so smart they skipped him two grades. The school principal said he'd watch after the younger boys, almost teenagers—surely, they will all be safe. She fears for her life. She is bound for her brother's one-room cabin in Chilliwack, with the baby in her arms and the baby in her belly, and the two other girls, bundled in their chubby cheeks and little parkas. But the boys, the boys are almost grown. How could she take them all?

*

Bob has spent weeks sleeping on the recliner in the living room, his bed too difficult to get out of. Now he can't get up for a smoke anymore, or the bathroom, and he finally agrees to go to the hospital. The nurses find what he has somehow hidden from everyone—bedsores grown to rotten flesh, falling off his body. Kent retells the story of the time his dad had all his teeth pulled without anaesthesia. He drove down to the dentist in Hinton from the work camp where he was, there was a snowstorm, he couldn't come back tomorrow. Just pull them, he said. We laugh at this story we know, while the nurses spend hours filling a garbage bag with dressings. And in his morphine sleep his face betrays him, admits the pain.

Kent and his brother and other loved ones keep a constant vigil at the bedside. But when Kent finally goes to sit with the kids in the unit's family room for a while, I find myself sitting alone with Bob. Impossible to tell if he is awake or asleep, impossible to tell if he knows I am here. Now there is no awkwardness in our silence. And for the first time I am free to stare at the body of this man that I love. His birthmark blooms out of the bed, not a bruise, not a spill, but a wealth of blood, capillaries defying the normal path. Saying, I have lived, I am still here, this is my skin.

From the hallway, my daughter's voice rings through the hush, a wordless laugh. She doesn't know why we are here or what is happening, just as she doesn't know the other great loss of her short life. The paediatrician says her mark is just a hemangioma; ninety percent disappear by the age of 10. But in her mark is my longing, that she will always carry something of him: his resilience, his capacity for love in spite of pain. And that she will live her life without ever needing these things. A memory, then, of choosing the most colourful stones and placing them in his open hand.

Drive-by

I am walking down my own street when I see them, two figures in the truck parked ahead. Her face is shrouded by her hair. His hand rests on her back but he stares forward, blank. I see them and then look away, pretend the windshield is the kind of shield they must be wishing for. The truck is red, the sidewalk is grey, my home is just there.

That fall day, driving home from the ultrasound clinic. Halfway home you pulled over, we held each other and cried. The still dark spot that had been our child had grown, filled the car, blocked the road, blocked the sky. The radio was playing "Take a Walk on the Wild Side." Who saw us then, bent together, shaking in each other's arms? What stories did those strangers see for us, what private griefs returned for them? What griefs rode past us in those cars, took the wheel, slammed down the gas?

I would like to open the door, crawl into that cab, curl up beside them.

I will walk away quickly, as if I didn't see.

Almost Behind Us

"I think he knocked out my tooth," I tell my husband, carefully feeling around my mouth with my tongue. M had been in my arms; he wanted to dance. As I put him down on the floor, he jumped too soon, colliding with my chin. It is the first anniversary of my mother's death.

My father is on his way over. A casual dinner on a Tuesday night, *we should be together on this day.* Nothing fancy or formal, but just this once, this first time. For thirty years he has sent his own mother flowers on the anniversary of his father's death. Mom had always thought this was morbid. She wouldn't have wanted us to mark her day like that. So, tacos—refried beans, grated cheese and flour tortillas. After-work chaos of a hungry kid on the hip held away from the splattering stove.

The tooth is pushed back into my mouth at a forty-five degree angle and wedged tight. Seeing me holding my face and my breath, M cries that he hurt his tooth too. He can't articulate his feelings, so they become physical pain. I am trying not to talk— everything is throbbing now—so Kent phones the emergency number on the dentist's voicemail, trying to figure out where we can go. M says, "I need to go to the dentist too." So I comfort him, check his teeth, the top of his head, tell him I'll be okay. Turn off the stove.

Dad arrives as he always does, with his slippers and a bottle of wine in a grocery bag. He sees my hand over my mouth.

"You both go," he says. "I'll watch the kids."

"I want to come with you!" M cries as we grab our jackets.

"Lucky I was here, today," Dad says.

*

The nearest dentist has another emergency case come in just before we arrive. So we drive north, phoning around, then east, finally ending up in a small clinic deep on the south side, explaining, "my son—he jumped." The dentist numbs me with a needle, and I think about the supper we left on the stove, whether my kids are in bed, whether I will lose my tooth. How my mother once kept my baby teeth in the drawer of her nightstand. How the feelings we can't articulate become physical pain. How the day stands not for the moment of loss, but the time that grief has been endured. *A whole year.* Or, *thirty years ago.* My father has already announced a new engagement. Couldn't you have waited a year, I wanted to say. Just until that first anniversary is behind us. But now it is almost behind us. "How old is your son?" the dentist is asking. "That was an awful lot of force." Yanking the tooth back in place.

*

I come home with a splint, which looks and feels like the braces I had when I was twelve. The kids are asleep; Dad is sitting with a glass of wine. He hands me a small jewellery box of gourmet chocolates, tied with a ribbon. "I can't eat them now," I say. "Only soft things. Maybe tomorrow." I don't realize until after he has gone that I should have opened them anyway, that he was waiting for me to share them. My mother would have loved these. Bergamot truffle, cardamom, chili. Not a gift but an offering, a way to acknowledge the things we aren't going to talk about. Her death, our grief, the time that has passed.

*

My family will not acknowledge that day again. But it will come—a Wednesday, a Thursday, a work night, a pork chop night. A whole year, since I last bit an apple.

I will have a root canal the next morning. Then, for a month, try to talk without my lip slipping above the splint. And when it does, I'll tell the story—my son, he wanted to dance.

Theory of Mind

I am about eight years old in the painting, smiling down at the kitten in my arms as if I am about to nuzzle my face into his fur. My mother painted it from a photograph, and it hung in my parents' house for so many years that, when I saw the original photo in an album—same angle of my head, same pink corduroy jumper—I could see the brushstrokes like an afterimage.

I have always hated this painting. Not because of its amateur realism, or my bowl-shaped haircut and ruffled collar. I hate this painting because it wasn't my cat. Because I never had a cat, never loved a cat. And the fact that people thought it was my cat, saw that little girl with her smile and told themselves stories about a beloved pet, a bond that did not exist, gave me a tightness in my throat, a kind of sadness.

I'm not an animal person. When I was eight, I may have wished for a cat, may have wished for *this* cat, but I don't remember doing so. I don't remember whose pet it was, or feeling the fondness painted on this face that was mine. My sadness doesn't come from some unrealized childhood love, but from the assumption other people have of that love. It is the queasiness of dishonesty, even in its least intentional, most inconsequential form.

There are many words for emotions that don't have an equivalent in English. *Fremdschämen*, German: to be embarrassed for someone else. *Gigil*, Tagalog: the irresistible desire to squeeze something cute. But I can't find a word in any language for this feeling, though it comes all the time. Strangers who think the frog stuffy in my son's arms is a beloved attachment object, rather than a toy he took with him today on a whim. My father thinking the red on my daughter's face is a wound, instead of raspberry.

As I wipe the jam off her forehead with my thumb, I am imagining that other reality, the one in which she fell on a toy, or walked into the corner of the table. I am imagining her crying, me comforting her, and the feeling rushes in like sadness. It's like a momentary recognition of one of millions of parallel lives we might have lived. Recognizable, ordinary, just not ours. It is not a wish that she had hurt herself, but it is a kind of nostalgia, a longing for a home that has been lost to the butterfly effects of life.

So, when M begins to lie to people about trivial things, I have to rush to set the record straight. No, he didn't really throw up at daycare. No, he's not allergic to chocolate. No, we didn't go swimming today. I can't let those parallel lives take shape in their minds or mine—his satisfied shiver, wrapping his dripping body in a kangaroo towel, a different way I could have mothered him today.

Preschoolers aren't compulsive liars in the clinical sense. He is testing out a new skill, experimenting with how much he can make grown-ups believe. He has developed what psychologists call "theory of mind," the recognition that others have different beliefs from your own, based on their own experience and knowledge. Lying is a developmental milestone, as the child realizes that they can manipulate the beliefs of others.

The development of theory of mind has been well researched. In an experiment known as the "false belief task," preschoolers are presented with a familiar box, such as a Smarties box. But when they open it, they discover that it contains pencils instead. Then another person is brought into the room, who hasn't seen inside the box. "What does this person think is in there?" the researchers ask the children. "Pencils!" the younger children say. They also say that before they opened the box, *they* thought there were pencils inside. They aren't yet capable of understanding that someone could have a belief that is different from reality, even if they did themselves, five minutes before.

But once they do make that realization, they are able to fib, to trick. The line between lying and imagination is too blurry for any parental discipline. But when I correct the record, I probably encourage M's deceptive behaviour, giving it more attention, more reaction.

His new theory of mind couldn't be big enough to recognize my emotion, that feeling that doesn't even have a name. The regret of trivial misrecognition. The discomfort of projected confabulation. Maybe I have an overdeveloped theory of mind, too much awareness that others have different beliefs about my life, and the ability to picture what they imagine. I also hate certain kinds of jokes. My husband pretending he quit his job when his boss returns from vacation. Friends in matching sweaters, posing for a mock Sears family portrait—if someone thought it was sincere! It is worst with children, and other heartstring-pulling tropes—animals, family mementos, anything innocent, anything sentimental. The fake member of my brother's university choir: not because he doesn't really exist, but because his name is the diminutive "Timmy."

*

Commouvere, Italian: a story's ability to move you. *Nunchi*, Korean: literally "eye-measure"; the ability to sense another's emotions. *Goya*, Urdu: "as if"; the alternate reality conjured by a good storyteller.

*

Since Mom died, the cat painting has been in my father's storage locker. Now he is getting remarried, and clearing out the things that were my mother's, the things that she made. He brings over boxes of playbills from shows she wrote or performed in, unreadable floppy disks, and I find a place for it all in my storage room. I hang other paintings of me as a kid in my own children's bedrooms. But I won't take the cat painting, though the thought of it in the landfill or a dark corner of the Goodwill, still telling its lies, is almost enough to make me keep it.

The feeling is almost unbearable when someone asks one of my children if their holiday was to visit Grandma. The fact that my children do not have living grandmothers is a wound that doesn't close; it is a different kind of wound when strangers think they do. It taps into the original loss like a vein, but the pain is in a different limb. The life that those strangers imagine for my kids: boarding a plane to visit Grandma in another province, wearing little backpacks with stuffies sticking out. Or maybe she lives here, and is one of the grandparents outnumbering parents at the playground, with tissues tucked inside sweatshirt cuffs, going down the slide with a toddler between her legs.

My father's new wife is too young to be my mother, but not too young to be my children's grandmother. It hasn't happened yet, that a stranger has spoken to my children and called her "your grandma." But it seems inevitable, the way that people stoop towards them in elevators, call my son young man, tell my daughter she has a kitty on her sweater, do you like kitties? Are you out with Grandma today? they will say, smiling, imagining the swing pushing, the ice cream treat. Erasing my children's loss.

*

Inscriptions in books at used bookstores also generate a similar feeling, especially those that flicker with lost lives or discarded loves. The picture books, now outgrown: *Merry Christmas, love Granny.* A little girl become a grown up, unsentimental about her childhood stories, and the grandmother who once read to her at bedtime. The book about schooners: *To Dad, I hope this reminds you of our times around the bay.* This time it is me, imagining another's life. What loss brought this book here? Why didn't the son take it back, after his father died? How could he get rid of it like that?

*

Vermod, Swedish: wistful sadness for something that is over. *Hiraeth*, Welsh: longing for something that may never have been.

*

When M first started talking about "my friend Sharon," we thought she was a girl, or maybe a parent volunteer, at preschool. But the teachers said there were no Sharons they knew. Then he told us she was an elephant.

Researchers have found that children who have imaginary friends develop theory of mind sooner. It gives them practice imagining the perspective of another person. Sharon appeared when M was almost three, the typical age for imaginary friends, when children often crave the companionship of a peer, but aren't yet equipped to make friends in the real world. Sharon lived in places he had heard of or that he pointed to on the globe—California, Colombia. "My friend Sharon is coming for dinner tonight," he'd inform us, but then leave it there. I never heard him talking to her; she was never blamed for spilling the cup. She was always absent, popping up in wild tales of motorcycle riding and swimming across the ocean, and in ordinary ways: "My friend Sharon's favourite colour is blue." Sometimes she was a kid, and sometimes she was very old. "She's not really an elephant, it was just a *costume*."

One evening we told him that our friends' dog had died. He had liked the dog, would have wondered where he was next time we visited. "My friend Sharon died, too," he said matter-of-factly.

"She did?"

"Yeah, she was being really silly and fell off the table and she hit her head really hard. So..." He shrugged his shoulders. "No more Sharon."

I choked, trying not to laugh. But then I stopped. This was death, to him. This was how it was when my mother died—she was here, then no more. I had told him calmly, hours after she passed, when my tears had dried. Then we watched a movie. We all tried to be normal so he wouldn't be scared. As his theory of mind was starting to develop, I failed to teach him grief.

It was true, there was no more Sharon. Whatever need for companionship or adventure had birthed her had been fulfilled. He didn't use Sharon's death to break the bounds of mortality—he seemed to understand its finality, and was committed to imposing the limits of reality, for once, onto his imagination.

*

Linguists and anthropologists have debated for centuries how language shapes our experience. Do people coin words for the feelings that are important in their culture, or do the words in a people's emotional lexicon shape what and how they feel? In the '70s American anthropologist Robert Levy, after spending two years in the Society Islands, coined the term "hypocognition," the lack of ability to comprehend a concept when you don't have a word for it. He racistly surmised that, because Tahitians seemed to lack words for sadness and grief, they had no way of dealing with it. The concept not only places an arrogant importance on English and western culture as the baseline for comparison, it assumes that the cultures that readily use the word "grief" can better understand it.

*

Now that they are getting married, my dad wants the kids to call his bride something besides Tina. They have been thinking about it—since she's Italian, maybe she could be Nona Tina? I am quiet for a long time, contemplating this. Will the kids accept it? What will they understand it to mean? She is good with them, gets down on the floor to race cars and build blocks, makes a game of cleaning up the toys. They love her already. It seems right, to give her a name of some sort. If people hear the kids call her Nona Tina at the park, will they be more or less likely to think she's their grandmother? Will they think we're Italian?

A few times lately, C has pointed to the guitar on top of the piano and said "Tina's guitar." The first time, I thought I must have misheard her. The second time, I was quick to correct her. "No, *Nanny's* guitar." It's the one my mother saved up to buy when she was sixteen, and taught herself to play. No one in my house knows how to play; it sits there as decoration, monument. But a week or two later, again, "Tina's guitar." I don't know if Tina once got it down, or talked about it with her one day, or if my baby has made some logical leaps. At two, she is just starting to learn the nature of relationships—that Uncle Grant is Mama's brother, that Poppy is Mama's daddy. She was only a few months old when Nanny died, but she has seen pictures. She knows Nanny was my mother. She knows Nanny was with Poppy. Now Tina is with Poppy. So Nanny must be Tina, or Tina must be Nanny.

"Nanny died," M tells his sister.

"Died?"

*

Mono no aware, Japanese: sadness that everything must end.
Saudade, Portuguese: the presence of absence.

*

They are at the park; they are being pushed on the swing. Do they feel love in the fingers on their back, or are they too focused on the air, the drop of gravity, the rushing past of the world? I want others to know my children's loss, in case they don't remember it themselves.

*

My dad brings over blank canvases and Mom's old brushes—maybe the kids would like to paint on these? I remember Mom letting me paint on a real canvas when I was small, wearing one of her old shirts as a smock, so long it brushed my ankles.

"Mom," M asks, "what is the saddest thing that happened to you?"

I remember, she showed me how to hold the brush, how to make a sky—first you paint the whole canvas blue, then later, when it's dry, you begin to layer on the horizon. You have to be patient, you have to build it over time. It is a sentimental image. But it really happened. This is a story I want to tell. This is a story I want painted on my face.

Maybe I will repeat the scene with my children. Maybe I will teach them new words: Canvas. Palette. Horizon.

Dreaming the Road

"The lake has its own weather. It could be sunny and hot in town, and as soon as you got out to the lake, it would be pouring."

We are winding along the gravel road, the section you call the chicanes, telling me it's all muskeg in here. We have been married fourteen years, and every time you bring me here is both the first and the hundredth. The lake is somewhere ahead, beyond the spruce, where the road drops down into the past. You are taking me there; I am attending your memory.

"There's a corner where the lake appears. That's where we knew what kind of day it would be. Thunderheads over the water. Or, sometimes, there'd be a break in the cloud, and the sun would be shining only on the lake."

In his car seat our son is sleeping. You want him to know this place too, the lake, the land where you grew up, pull of muskeg on his boots, pull of the woods, the open hands of spruce. This morning he was covered scalp to sole in raspberries. You held him back from the bucket, but your uncle said, "no, let him go." Filling his fists and mouth with the taste, discovery of tart and sweet, skin stained the pink of newness.

You want him to know this part of you, to lean his head there. The smell of iron and rain.

"I have slept this road many times," you tell me. An unusual phrasing, a poetic phrasing. You mean that, after a day of fishing, you would fall asleep in the truck, lightly, the window cool against your temple, as your dad drove. Eyes closed, your body knew every bend. Now, your dad is following behind in his own truck, your own son is sleeping, we are arriving, not returning.

You have dreamt this road many times since. In cities where the traffic always kept you awake beside me, in cities with their own weather, warmed by cars and concrete. You coughed on the dust from the truck that just passed, smelled the iron of the fish on your skin and clothes. Heard the crackle of the gravel on the undercarriage, like popping corn.

Later, our son will pick the tall grass beneath the picnic table. Later you will show him a fish, and he will grab at the scales shining in the sunlight. Try to put it in his mouth, tiny fingers smeared with blood.

"When I die you should bury me in muskeg, then you can visit me whenever you want. I'll be preserved."

"Like the bog man in Denmark!"

Later, we will go down with a daughter sitting in the back beside our son. We have been married twenty years, your dad is gone. We are going again, down to the lake, to your memory, the hundredth time, the first. You point to the trees, thick as fingers. "It's all muskeg in here."

I read that in the bogs of Europe they found not only ancient bodies but butter, wrapped in skin, as if the bog were a fridge in the ground. We will swim in the water made the colour of tea by the muskeg that surrounds it. The smooth hide of the lake stretched over its working muscle. Then, a shift of angle, and the light will flash on the little waves, paparazzi to our beautiful life.

Later our children will dream of the gravel spit, the slope of sky through the rear windows. The turn of the road in the belly, the last deep bend. The sky smeared pink.

Exhausted from a day in the sun, the rhythm of the gravel and the rocking of the tires in the ruts, you didn't need to keep your eyes open.

"I know every curve of this road."

We round the corner. There's a break in the cloud beyond the lake, just above the tree line. In the back, our son's chin has rolled low against his chest. Every bend is new to me, but he, he is sleeping the road, all the days to come.

"This trip was already worth it, for the raspberries."

Notes

The biblical scholar referenced in "Micrographia" is Jeremy D. Smoak, whose article "Words Unseen: The Power of Invisible Writing" appears in the January/February 2018 issue of *Biblical Archaeology Review*.

The poem referenced in "Screen Time" is Sharon Olds' "Looking at Them Asleep" in *Strike Sparks: Selected Poems, 1980-2002*.

Italicized lines in "Passage" are from Bill C-14, *An Act to Amend the Criminal Code and to make Related Amendments to Other Acts (medical assistance in dying)*, 2016.

The italicized lines in "Spectre" are from Giovanni Caputo, "Strange-face-in-the-mirror illusion," *Perception* 39, 2010.

Lines in "The Dance" are from Elizabeth Bowering's unpublished plays *Wind at Her Sails* and *The Dance*.

Acknowledgments

This book was written in ◁┌ᶰᖯ·ᒉ·◁·ᶰᖯ‖Δᖯᓄ Amiskwaciwâskahikan, in Treaty 6 and Métis Region 4, gathering place for diverse Indigenous peoples including the Cree, Blackfoot, Métis, Nakota Sioux, Iroquois, Dene, Ojibway/Saulteaux/Anishinaabe, Inuit, and many others; and on the unceded territory of the xʷməθkʷəy̓əm (Musqueam), Sḵwx̱wú7mesh (Squamish), and səlilwətaɬ (Tsleil-Waututh) First Nations. I am honoured to create in these places, and attempt to do so with respect, humility and gratitude.

I am grateful to the many readers and friends who provided generous feedback on the work included here, particularly Claire Kelly, Lisa Martin, Wendy McGrath, and Matthew Stepanic. Thanks also to friends who workshopped early pieces: Sonnet L'Abbé, Mandy Len Catron, Ken Klonsky, Nilofar Shidmehr, and Janey Lew. Thanks to Grant Bowering for giving feedback from the perspective of both reader and brother. Lorri Neilsen Glenn's editing, advice, and encouragement early on were critical to the development of this book. Thanks, finally, to Shane Neilson for believing in this book and pushing me to make it better.

Thanks to the editors who published versions of these pieces:
"A Routine Test" in *Brain, Child*
"Micrographia" in *The Malahat Review*
"Peonies" and "In Pleasantview Cemetery" in *Contrary*
"Abracadabra" in *The Forge*
"Passage" in *The Antigonish Review*
"Almost Behind Us" in *Creative Nonfiction's Sunday Short Reads*
"Theory of Mind" in *The Fiddlehead*.
Particular thanks to Alicia Elliott and Valerie Waterhouse.

I am grateful to have received funding for this project from the Canada Council, the Alberta Foundation for the Arts, and the Edmonton Arts Council.

Thanks to all of the loved ones who appear in these pages for being part of my life and my work. Love and gratitude to Annette Resler for her generosity with her story.

Thanks to my mother, Elizabeth Bowering, for everything she taught me, from the first word to the last.

Thanks, finally, to my children and my husband, for their love and support.

About the Author

Jennifer Bowering Delisle is the author of a poetry collection, *Deriving* (2021) and a lyric family memoir, *The Bosun Chair* (2017). She has a PhD in English and frequently teaches creative writing classes and workshops. She is also a board member of NeWest Press. She lives in Edmonton/Amiskwaciwâskahikan/ Treaty 6 where she is an instructional designer and a mother of two. Find her online @JenBDelisle and www.jenniferdelisle.ca.